BUILDING A WINNING CURRICULUM

How *to* Use Vision Forum Products *to* Build *a* Winning Homeschool Curriculum

By Dorys Lee Horn

THIRD PRINTING
COPYRIGHT © 2011 THE VISION FORUM, INC.
All Rights Reserved

"Where there is no vision, the people perish." (Proverbs 29:18)

The Vision Forum, Inc.
4719 Blanco Rd., San Antonio, Texas 78212
www.visionforum.com

Compiled by Jeff and Dorys Lee Horn

Cover Design by Austin Collins
Typography by Justin Turley

PRINTED IN THE UNITED STATES OF AMERICA

TABLE OF CONTENTS

INTRODUCTION

When my wife and I made the decision in 1989 to homeschool our then five-year-old son, we had no idea what a priority home education would become in our lives. Quite frankly, we are not alone. Home education is an important topic to a significant number of people, and that number is growing dramatically.

The questions often asked by those involved in home education, or contemplating the process, are:

"What exactly is home education?"

"What is the process supposed to look like?"

"How should I go about this process, and what materials should I use?"

Home education can look very different from family to family. However, the biblical underpinnings are really the same for all of us. It involves so much more than reading, writing, and arithmetic. At its core, homeschooling consists of parents training the next generation and bringing them up in the nurture and admonition of the Lord. To do this effectively, we as parents must help to cast a vision for our children, establishing patterns and developing themes which will prepare our sons and daughters to be strong in the faith and equipped to lead Christ-centered lives.

Vision Forum is committed to aiding parents in their journey down this essential road, and has produced a wealth of resources—written, visual and audio—during the past decade to help families fulfill this commitment. Countless families, including ours, have made use of these offerings, and in so doing have received tremendous blessings. Yet a common refrain is often heard:

"How can I make these products a part of my home educating curriculum?"

In response to this question, the goal of this guide is to systematically present a number of resources offered by Vision Forum that families can use to build their own winning homeschool curricula. Our idea is to provide substantive discussion of the materials, as well as insightful suggestions by my wife, who has been teaching our children at home for over twenty years, on how to use these products as part of the home education process in your family. Naturally, there will be many other ways to utilize the books, DVDs and CDs beyond the ideas listed here, but it is our prayer that these suggestions will serve to stimulate additional thoughts among those who read this guide. Although the vast majority of Vision Forum-produced products are covered in this guide, due to space limitations some have not been included. Remember that these products are not an end unto themselves, but rather tools which the Lord can use as we seek to train our children for His glory.

Jeff Horn
San Antonio, Texas

PART I
SETTING THE VISION FOR HOME EDUCATION

And these words, which I command thee this day, shall be in thine heart: And thou shalt teach them diligently unto thy children, and shalt talk of them when thou sittest in thine house, and when thou walkest by the way, and when thou liest down, and when thou risest up. —Deuteronomy 6: 6-7

If you are beginning this journey, or just seeking to refresh your home education vision, remember that the overall atmosphere and order of daily life provides the structure for all that takes place in the home. As fathers and mothers demonstrate their God-given roles, and as families develop harmonious relationships, family life becomes the foundation for the home educating process. A few of our favorite Vision Forum resources that have helped our family work toward meeting these goals will be included in this section, together with suggestions on how to use them most effectively as you seek to set the vision for your home education.

Commentary & Product Review

A Home School Vision of Victory

Listening to this message by Doug Phillips with a friend who had been homeschooling for years, I will never forget her exclamation, "Now I understand why I am doing this!" It was truly a life-changing moment for this woman as she refreshed her vision and purposed to stay the course. An excellent resource for those new to homeschooling or those desiring to renew their vision.

Format: CD

Resource for: Parents

An Encouragement: Do your children know why you are teaching them at home? Sometimes in the busyness of life, we assume that our purposes are clear. Why not take an evening to listen to this talk with your children and discuss the points made by Mr. Phillips?

The Visionary Father's Role in Home Education

Defining what the role of the father should be in home education, and giving personal examples and encouragement to fathers, Doug Phillips lays out seven components of a father's role in discipling his children. Highly recommended for dads desiring to fulfill their biblical role of shepherd over their home.

Format: CD

Resource for: Men

Family Man, Family Leader

This book, written by Phil Lancaster, is my husband's favorite resource on encouraging men to lead their families. Providing the vision and tools to achieve family renewal, Mr. Lancaster shows men how to turn their hearts toward home. Asserting the truth that God Himself is a father, and the importance of fathers as servant-leaders, a compelling case is made for the rebuilding of the family. The principles and wisdom found in this book are vital to the life of the home educating father.

Format: Book

Resource for: Men

An Encouragement: Do you need some godly exhortation? How about some suggestions on leading your family to be better prepared for the home educating process? Do you know someone just beginning to consider homeschooling? This book is a great resource!

The Wise Woman's Guide to Blessing Her Husband's Vision

Home educating mothers can easily become discouraged when they think that their husbands lack vision or do not share in their desire to follow biblical principles. Addressing this issue with compassion and wisdom, Doug Phillips explains the roles of both husband and wife and encourages women to respond to their husbands in a biblical manner. I recommend this message for all women desiring to be a sanctifying influence on their homes as they seek to find ways to bless their husbands. No better foundation can be laid for the home educating family than for a wife to teach her children to honor their father.

Format: CD (2)

Resource for: Women

An Encouragement: Why not invite a few fellow homeschooling mothers over for an evening of fellowship and encouragement and listen to this CD by Mr.

Phillips? Having a mom in harmony with her role as wife will be one of the best ways to begin a school year.

Large Family Logistics: The Art and Science of Managing the Large Family

As a mother of nine children, Kim Brenneman knows the challenges that come with homeschooling a large family. Offering a sensible and straightforward approach to home management, Kim provides problem-solving "how tos" for mothers that can be applied to families of all sizes. From this book you will learn how to:

- Fit Everything into a Day
- Organize Your Week
- Conquer the Laundry Monster
- Take Control of Your Clutter
- Establish Solid Morning and Evening Routines
- Develop Easy Menu Plans
- Restart Your Day When Things Go Wrong
- Save Money at the Grocery Store
- Maximize Bedroom and Closet Space
- Organize Your Kitchen for Maximum Efficiency

Isn't it wonderful when someone who has gone before us is willing to share the lessons learned along the way? This book should be used as a "Mama's Manual" for each and every day!

Format: Book

Resource for: Women of all ages

An Encouragement: Use this book as a practical manual for home economics. The topics lend themselves to areas of study for daughters in preparation for motherhood and homemaking.

The Family

Few books have impacted my vision of the sanctified life as this one has. Originally published in 1882, *The Family* shows the God-given design for the home. Describing each relationship in the family from a biblical perspective, Rev. J.R. Miller lovingly encourages each of us to find purpose and joy in our specific family roles. Well suited for husbands and wives to read together.

Format: Book

Resource for: Parents and young adults

An Encouragement: If Christian families could be the "fragrance of the Lord Jesus" to others as described in The Family, *we would be well on our way to being world changers. What a wonderful foundation for any home economics course. A definite read for all my adult children before leaving our home.*

Victories! Moments, Large and Small, Which Define Christian Parenthood

Join Doug Phillips as he reminds parents of the everyday joys found in parenthood. Sharing from personal experience and from the lives of families in history, Mr. Phillips outlines the often overlooked victories of parenting. As busy home educating parents, we can easily become insensitive to the beauty of our everyday lives. Be encouraged as you seek to recapture and appreciate your family culture and enjoy the blessings God has given you!

Format: CD

Resource for: Parents

An Encouragement: Have you ever had "one of those days?" You know the kind, where the "everyday" seems a bit overwhelming? We all need a reminder now and again of the incredible blessing of this parenting season of life. This talk will bring refreshment to your heart.

Identity Theft: Why Our Children's Identities Are Being Stolen by the World, and What We Can Do about It

Do you realize that the world is vying for the affections of your children? With whom do they identify? Doug Phillips warns all parents through this message to be aware of how the culture impacts and affects all children, *even* those who are home educated. Grappling with the issues of our time, Mr. Phillips encourages parents to make identification with Christ the priority. A friend of ours distributed this message to his fellow church members because he heeded the warning and wanted others to do so as well. Listen to this convicting talk to be sure your parenting is not being undermined.

Format: CD (2)

Resource for: Parents and children

Toxic: Seven Poisons that Threaten the Health of the Homeshool Movement—and Their Antidotes

Listen as Doug Phillips outlines these seven deadly threats that seek to undermine the health of the homeschool community. Be prepared to defend the spiritual health of your own children as Mr. Phillips provides antidotes for parents to use against these poisons infecting our churches and homes.

Format: CD

Resource for: Parents and children

An Encouragement: It is so helpful for our children to understand why we make the choices we do. Listen to Identity Theft *and* Toxic *with your family and discuss the cautions and solutions to the cultural challenges of our day. Let your children listen to this message, and then have them give a speech, illustrated with some of their own experiences, about this important topic.*

How and Why to Work with Your Children (Set)

d *Tilling the Soil: Cultivating an Entrepreneurial Vision in Your Family*
2. *Getting Your Hands Dirty: How to Teach Your Children to Love Work*

These audio messages recorded by Joel Salatin at the Entrepreneurial Bootcamp are foundational resources for parents with children of almost any age. Teaching and encouraging our children to be enthusiastic workers at home has always been one of our home educating goals. In these messages, Mr. Salatin, himself a part of a multi-generational farming enterprise, shares insights and ideas gleaned from years of experience. Included with his "how to get children to work" tips are ideas on how to integrate children into every aspect of your family business. Although these materials are from an agrarian perspective, the information can be easily adapted to fit almost any home or family business situation. I highly recommend these CDs to all parents!

Format: CD (2)

Resource for: Parents

An Encouragement: Wondering how to integrate your family business with your home educating? Want to know how to get your children to embrace your family vision? Just want some ideas on how to make everyday chores more fun? Listen to these talks and find satisfaction in your everyday family life!

The Promise: The Beauty and Power of the Fifth Commandment

What better way to start off a new year of home educating than by watching or listening to this message by Doug Phillips. Do your children understand the value and blessing of giving honor to all those in authority? Providing scriptural support, as well as biblical and personal examples, Mr. Phillips encourages us to impact our culture by being families who demonstrate honor. Topical chapter divisions are included in the menu options of this DVD, making it well suited for personal Bible study. Available on CD as well.

Format: DVD and CD

Resource for: Family

An Encouragement: Do your children understand why we seek to establish our homes with respectful communication? Do you have questions about how to honor your family and friends who may not be agreeing with your home education? Use this DVD to establish biblical communication principles for your home, and see the blessings that come to your family as you honor God's ways.

PART 2
BUILDING A WINNING CURRICULUM

And, ye fathers, provoke not your children to wrath: but bring them
up in the nurture and admonition of the Lord. —Ephesians 6:4

One of the many advantages to home education is the opportunity to provide a unique course of study, tailor-made to the circumstances, life goals, character training, and academic pursuits of individual families. As my husband and I sought to bring up our children in the nurture and admonition of the Lord, we wanted to build a curriculum that would provide our children not only with opportunities to demonstrate academic achievement, but also Christ-like character. This next section will provide some ideas on how to compose a framework for your studies and choice of materials as you seek to build a winning curriculum through:

Comments and *Curriculum Advice* Review

Ideas for Building a Unit Study

A Biblical Worldview

Comments &
Curriculum Advice Review

As you read through this guide to find materials to build your homeschool curriculum, you will also discover creative ways to use each resource. Although many of the ideas presented in this guide focus on the older student, younger children may also benefit by listening to and viewing many of the Vision Forum resources. While your older children are taking notes, younger ones can be doing hands-on activities such as: puzzles, hand-sewing projects, coloring and drawing. For a more focused approach for younger children, try using flashcards with vocabulary words from the resource or simple questions that can be discovered and answered by watching the film or listening to the audio presentation. When these words are "discovered," or the answer given, pause the resource and use that time for discussion. Although an attempt has been made to provide appropriate age-levels recommendations, most resources can used by the whole family with parental oversight.

The following resource, **Curriculum Advice: Volumes 1 and 2,** although not a Vision Forum-produced product, is included here as an excellent overview of how to best "build a winning curriculum."

Curriculum Advice: Volume 1

Are you concerned you may not be "qualified" to teach your own children? Do you want a simple plan for how to home educate your younger children, ages 3 through 8? Do you know how to set a positive, God-honoring atmosphere in your own home? Victoria Botkin shares with great insight, compassion, and creativity the "whys" and "how tos" of teaching your children at home. With an introduction by her husband, Geoff, and fascinating commentary by several of her seven children, this talk provides a framework for your beginning home education experience.

Format: CD

Resource for: Parents

Curriculum Advice: Volume 2

As a companion to Volume 1 or as a stand-alone resource, this talk on how to home educate children eight years or older is invaluable. Making suggestions on how to teach subjects such as math, language arts, geography, history and science, Mrs. Botkin seeks to make the home education process an integral part of a dynamic and hospitable home life. Counsel for the wife whose husband has little time for, or interest in, homeschooling is also provided. What makes this talk so unique is the commentary by Victoria's seven children about how they have been profoundly impacted by their mother and her home education philosophy!

Format: CD

Resource for: Parents

Additional Vision Forum Resources

> *Of Plymouth Plantation* (book), by William Bradford
>
> G.A. Henty Historical Fiction Series, by G.A. Henty
>
> R.M. Ballantyne Christian Adventure Library, by R.M. Ballantyne

An Encouragement: So, pour yourself a cup of tea or coffee and take some time to listen to these talks from Victoria. Her heartfelt compassion for the home educating mother is evident as she shares how she and her husband Geoff have made their home a source of life-giving education. Her ideas and wisdom provide not only encouragement, but also practical and economical ways in which to find resources that will enhance your own home education studies.

Ideas for Building a Unit Study

Before you begin to build a winning curriculum, it is helpful to identify specific goals to help you achieve this purpose. The following outline is a simple way to build a study from any subject or topic you may choose.

1. Set family, spiritual, and academic goals:
   What do you want to accomplish through this study?

2. Connect the topic of study to Scripture:
   What verses or biblical principles are foundational to this study?

3. Investigate your own personal library and/or media collection:
   What resources do you have on hand to complement this study?

4. Check out VisionForum.com:
   What additional materials are available that are not included in this guide?

5. Research the topic online and/or at the library:
   What supplementary materials can be found using inter-library loan?

6. Plan field trips that will enhance your study:
   Take vacations that include visits to historical sites. Vision

Forum Ministries Faith & Freedom Tours are an excellent source of hands-on history from a biblical perspective.

7. Read and enjoy historical books on the topic:
   What was it like to live during the time period?

8. Provide opportunities to discuss lessons learned:
   How did this study foster personal growth in the life of your family?

Building a Winning Curriculum Through a Biblical Worldview

My husband and I want all the learning that takes place in our family to be based on a biblical worldview. Because of this, we approach our teaching of academics by first determining how the resources we use fit into our worldview goals. For your convenience, I have organized the Vision Forum resources that will aid in the development of a **Biblical Worldview** into the following categories:

Apologetics and Evangelism

Christianity and Culture: Theology and Evangelism (pg. 145)

Character and Leadership

Defending the Faith through Manly Leadership (pg. 37)

Defending the Faith by Rebuilding a Culture of Virtuous Boyhood and Girlhood (pg. 61)

Defending the Faith through the Nobility of Womanhood (pg. 47)

Setting the Vision for Home Education (pg. 11)

Economics

Christianity and Culture: Business and Commerce (pg. 169)

Government and Law

Christianity and Culture: Government and Law (pg. 153)

History

Defending the Faith through the History of Christianity and Western Civilization (pg. 79)

Defending the Faith through Manly Leadership (pg. 37)

Home Engineering

Christianity and Culture: Family Life and Discipleship (pg. 135)

Defending the Faith through the Blessing of Children (pg. 55)
Setting the Vision for Home Education (pg. 9)

Literature and the Arts

Christianity and Culture: The Art of Film (pg. 159)

Defending the Faith by Rebuilding a Culture of Virtuous Boyhood and Girlhood (pg. 61)

Science

Defending the Faith through Science and Creationism (pg. 119)

PART 3
DEFENDING THE FAITH

Therefore brethren, stand fast and hold the traditions which ye have been taught, whether by word, or our epistle. —*2 Thessalonians 2:15*

One of the primary objectives of our home education journey has been to prepare our children to be defenders of the faith. Consequently, we have sought to provide opportunities and materials that would encourage and teach our children how to take stands for biblical truth. The resources included in this section will help your family be better prepared to defend the faith through:

Manly Leadership

The Nobility of Womanhood

The Blessing of Children

A Culture of Virtuous Boyhood and Girlhood

The Development of Christianity and Western Civilization

Science and Creationism

Manly Leadership

Because we have purposed to ensure that our children understand the biblical roles of manhood and womanhood as defined by God in His Word, and to make these principles foundational to all the character education our children receive, we have sought to build our curriculum with materials that enhance these truths. The following materials will provide encouragement for your family as you seek to develop an understanding of the necessity for manly leadership in our society.

Using the Vision Forum resource *Why Christian Manhood Must Prevail,* and including other resources that further expound upon this message, I have designed a sample study that you can use to teach your children a biblical understanding of manhood incorporating the study into an academic exercise. Hopefully this example will give you ideas for how you can turn other Vision Forum resources into full-fledged study units as well.

Why Christian Manhood Must Prevail

In this message, Doug Phillips explores the fall of Christian manhood over the past 100 years. Feminine masculinization and male effeminization have taken their toll on American society, helping to degrade the moral consciousness of our nation. But there is hope! As Mr. Phillips demonstrates through a multitude of historical and biblical examples, Christian men can still stand against the culture and obey the biblical command of male headship, protecting and nurturing women as Christ protects and nurtures His bride, the church.

Format: CD

Resource for: Age 10 to adult

An Encouragement: *After listening to this CD, begin a unit study on Christian manhood. Using online and library research, and any of the resources listed below, study the impact and influence on history men have had who were willing to live faithful lives of vision and leadership. Some categories for your study could be men functioning as:*

> ***Family Leaders***
>
> ***Household Historians***
>
> ***Spiritual Shepherds***
>
> ***Defenders of Women and Children***

Be sure to include a study of the men of the Bible who have given us the blueprint for manliness such as Joseph, Daniel, David, Paul, and of course the Lord Jesus Christ.

Additional Vision Forum Resources

> *The Sinking of the Titanic and Great Sea Disasters* (book), by Marshall Logan
>
> *The Birkenhead Drill* (book), by Doug Phillips
>
> *Women and Children First!* (CD), by Doug Phillips
>
> *The Heroism of the Fathers is the Legacy of the Sons* (CD), by Doug Phillips
>
> *Poems for Patriarchs* (book), compiled by Doug Phillips
>
> *The Role of Grandfathers in the Local Church* (CD), by Doug Phillips
>
> *Manliness* (CD), by Doug Phillips
>
> *Manly Friendships* (CD), by Doug Phillips
>
> *What Hollywood Teaches About Manhood* (CD), by Dr. Voddie Baucham
>
> *Defending the Fatherless* (CD), by Doug Phillips
>
> *Sergeant York and the Great War* (book), edited by Tom Skeyhill and

"Little Bear" Wheeler

Subjects: U.S. History, World History, Language Arts, Literature

Ideas for Composition and Discussion

Read *The Sinking of the Titanic* and *The Birkenhead Drill*. Describe the lives and character of the men who gave their lives for the women and children in these ships.

Define the Cowboy Code.

Use Scripture references to describe a Man of God.

Examine the changing perspective on the nobility of women in *Bradwell* vs. *The State of Illinois*

Analyze the moderin media culture and its impact on manhood

Further Study

John Jacob Astor

Archibald Butt

Pastor John Harper

Winston Churchill

Theodore Roosevelt

Margaret Sanger

John Dewey

Suffragettes

World War I

World War II

September 11, 2001

Following are reviews of the additional Vision Forum resources for this unit study.

The Sinking of the Titanic and Great Sea Disasters

"Women and children first!" The cry rang out upon the slanting deck amid screams and shouts of fright, as the largest ship in the world settled into her watery grave. The dark sea waves washed higher and higher on her metal sides, but the men on board stuck silently to their task: the women and children must be saved! At last the lifeboats left her side, with a chorus of groans and tears. Slowly but surely the vast hull sank into the cold Atlantic waters with her shipload of brave but doomed men. Thus departed the *Titanic*, a tragedy of epic proportions that has captivated millions by its story of heroism and manhood.

Format: Book

Resource for: Family (Reading level age 12 to adult)

The Birkenhead Drill

Few today know the story of the English troopship *Birkenhead*, as the more famous fate of the *RMS Titanic* has overshadowed the *Birkenhead's* testimony of sacrifice and bravery. This should not be. On February 26, 1852, the troopship *Birkenhead* struck an uncharted rock off the coast of Africa and foundered. She had few lifeboats, and of those, many were not in working order. The women were loaded into these boats and set upon the water while the British soldiers stood at silent attention on the sinking deck. The ship's captain shouted that they must jump overboard and swim to the boats, but the commanding officer realized that this would swamp the small lifeboats and kill the women and children. He ordered the men to stand steady, and all but a few cowards obeyed. Most of the men drowned or were eaten by great white sharks, their deaths a testimony to the cry of "Women and children first!" which would be uttered on the decks of the Titanic sixty years later. *The Birkenhead Drill* contains a narrative of the disaster, along with first-hand accounts, a comparison to the *Titanic*, the legend of the *Birkenhead's* lost cargo of gold, and more.

Format: Book

Resource for: Family (Reading level is age 12 to adult)

Women and Children First!

In the context of relating the heroic sacrifice of the men aboard the *Titanic*, Doug Phillips persuasively maintains that the biblical concept of saving women and children first remains relevant in our modern world. Filled with fascinating tidbits about the most famous shipwreck in history, this message encourages sons to honor their mothers and protect their sisters.

Format: CD

Resource for: Family

The Heroism of the Fathers is the Legacy of the Sons

Stories of heroism and bravery strike a sympathetic chord with me. I love to learn about the great deeds of the past, where men sacrificed their "lives, … fortunes, and … sacred Honor" (to quote the Declaration of Independence). This message is recorded from a night dedicated to remembering the sinking of the ships *Titanic* and *Birkenhead*, and the noble sacrifices of their passengers. Speaker Doug Phillips exposes the multigenerational legacy of heroism among the families of men such as United States President Theodore Roosevelt, and the soldier and Boy Scouts founder Lord Baden Powell. Prepare to be inspired!

Format: CD (2)

Resource for: Family

Poems for Patriarchs

Poetry and manhood? Yes! This collection of verse and prose provides a vision-producing assortment of materials for memorizing and reading aloud. This is poetry that men and boys can sink their teeth into! There are stirring poems of heroism and bravery, patriotic poems that speak of love of country, and reflective works that touch on sonship and fatherhood. Use *Poems for Patriarchs* as a study of poetry or as a complement to other subjects. Assign a selection and provide an accompanying verse of Scripture for memorization and meditation. What about hosting an evening of poetry for your family and or friends? Read the book's introduction for inspiration on why you need to make poetry an integral part of your curriculum.

Format: Book

Resource for: Family (Reading level is age 10 to adult)

The Role of Grandfathers in the Local Church

One of the blessings of home educating our children is to be able to help them think multigenerationally. Any study of Christian manhood should include the role of the man with the "hoary" head. In this message, Doug Phillips will encourage your sons to be prepared for all the stages of life and to realize that how they spend their days now will impact their role someday as a grandfather in the local church.

Format: CD

Resource for: Family

Manly Friendships

Why is there such a dearth of hearty, manly friendships in the Church today? Doug Phillips suggests it is because of the influence of the contemporary vision of manhood: the machismo man, the effeminate man, the angry man, etc. This talk takes us back to the biblical text for an honest review of manly friendships. The relationship of David and Jonathan serves as the springboard for understanding what true manly friendships look like, why they are so rare, and what men must do to achieve them.

Format: CD

Resource for: Age 12 to adult

Manliness

The case for embracing the biblical doctrine of manliness is boldly made by Doug Phillips in this message. He forcefully explains the biblical imperative that men must do their duty in the face of danger and even death. With insights from Teddy Roosevelt, the *Titanic* and Winston Churchill, Doug Phillips presents a clear charge to the men of our day: "Be thou strong therefore, and shew thyself a man" (I Kings 2:2).

Format: CD

Resource for: Age 10 to adult

What Hollywood Teaches About Manhood

Excerpts from Hollywood films old and new are deftly used to illustrate biblical qualities of manhood with both positive and negative examples. Dr. Voddie Baucham identifies from Genesis certain essential aspects of biblical manhood and compares and contrasts them with characters from movies such as: *Mr. Smith Goes to Washington, A Few Good Men,* and *Gladiator.* Dr. Baucham strongly warns against the danger of just watching films as entertainment without analyzing and understanding the worldview of the director and the characters he presents.

Format: CD

Resource for: Age 10 to adult

Defending the Fatherless

The clarion call for the Church to minister to the legitimate needs of single-mother homes is sounded by Doug Phillips as he reviews the scriptural criteria for pursuing this responsibility. Rejecting the modern solutions of statist welfare and placing mothers in the workplace as unbiblical, Mr. Phillips emphasizes the vital importance of the Church enabling single mothers to home educate their children.

Format: CD

Resource for: Age 10 to adult

Sergeant York and the Great War

When most people think of the unassuming hero Alvin York, they think of Gary Cooper's brilliant portrayal in the 1941 film *Sergeant York*. The story of this backwoods Tennessean is so truly remarkable that, even after discounting Hollywood's exaggerations, he remains an amazing testimony to God's providence. Alvin York was raised "hog wild," as he says in this edited autobiography, and grew up drinking, cursing, and fighting. His life completely changed, however, when he came to a saving knowledge of Jesus Christ. *Sergeant York and the Great War* is largely written by York himself, but also includes pictures and the history of World War I.

Format: Book

Resource for: Age 12 to adult

The League of Grateful Sons

When thousands of Marines stormed the black volcanic beaches of Iwo Jima on February 19, 1945, the resulting havoc was both spiritual and physical. Many of the soldiers who survived those bloody days were hardened by what they experienced, never sharing about their actions with their families. In *The League of Grateful Sons*, a group of these veterans travel back to Iwo Jima with their children and grandchildren by their sides as they recall the providences of God during the battle. It's a tear-wrenching sight to see these grey-haired soldiers relive the experiences of their youth, viewing the very ground upon which they lost so many comrades and exemplifying the need for parents to share about their lives with their descendants.

Format: DVD

Resource for: Family

An Encouragement: Why not study Iwo Jima, the Japanese fortifications, the actual battle, and the effects this battle had on the course of World War II?

Additional Vision Forum Products

Bible Lessons for Manhood from the Battlefield of My Father's Youth (6 CDs)

Jonathan Park Vol. 4: The Hunt for Beowulf (4 CDs)

#1: "The Return to Iwo Jima"

Coming In on a Wing and a Prayer

Kelly Bradrick (née Brown) writes this book in the style of a grandmother speaking to her grandchildren, recounting a real-life event from the life of her grandfather, P-51 Mustang fighter pilot Bill Brown. As a young man during World War II, Bill saw the carnage of Iwo Jima first-hand, landing on the blood-stained beaches as soon as possible to begin his flying missions. During one of his raids, Bill's plane was damaged by the enemy, forcing him to parachute into the Pacific Ocean. He spent several hours floating in an inflated life raft, praying that God would protect him from the Japanese. In God's remarkable providence, after Bill had spent many hours alone on the salty waves an American submarine surfaced and rescued him. Now an older man, Bill Brown continues to tell his grandchildren the stories of God's hand in his life, a legacy carried on by Kelly for her descendants.

Format: Book

Resource for: Family (Reading level is age 10 to adult)

The Nobility of Womanhood

Along with seeking to equip our daughters with the skills of academic excellence, we should also be sure they have a vision for godly womanhood. As parents, we can help them understand the privilege and responsibility that comes with the honor of being made female in God's design by providing resources that proclaim, define, and demonstrate these qualities.

Using the book *Verses of Virtue*, and going section by section, I have provided an example of how to design a study on the nobility of womanhood, and have included additional related Vision Forum resources as well. The reviews for each of the additional products will be included within each section.

Verses of Virtue

The premise of this book is clearly stated in its introduction: "Poetry is one of God's ordained means for communicating vision and helping us to retain our focus as women of purpose and mission." The book itself is a wonderful collection of poetry, seasoned with poignant prose, compiled and edited by Elizabeth Beall Phillips and organized into sections defining noble womanhood.

Format: Book

Resource for: Family (Reading level is age 10 to adult)

Subjects: Home Economics, Literature, Poetry, History

Each major section of Verses of Virtue *will be addressed as a topic of study in the following study sample.*

Visions of Virtue: (*Verses of Virtue* pp. 3-9)

Use Proverbs 31 as your scriptural basis for this study discussion and for memorization and handwriting practice. Within the context of this study the following areas can also be addressed:

Sewing and Needle Arts

Cooking

Entrepreneurial Business Skills

Physical Education

Servant Ministry

Personal Relationships

The article "Home: The Fountain-Head of Society," found in this section, can be used as the impetus for a study of the family throughout history. Another approach would be to use this article as a springboard for a biblical study on the decorating of a home. Continue analyzing and exploring the other selections for further study, discussion, and memorization.

Hearth and Home: (*Verses of Virtue* pp.13-18)

This section's introduction provides an excellent overview of how present-day home life has deviated from being the bastion of Christian society. What an exciting framework for further study on God's design of the home and the glories that come from living a life of noble womanhood! The poems and prose throughout "hearth and Home" can be used in a variety of ways, again with memorization, handwriting, illustrating and as benchmarks for writing and discussion. "A Christian Home" by Barbara B. Hart is my favorite of all hymns and can be an added musical resource.

The Bride (*Verses of Virtue* pp. 31-44)

By helping our daughters see the beauty of godly marriage, we also instruct them on the preciousness of the Bride, (the Church) to Christ. This section provides a beautiful overview of marriage. The historical poems "Evangeline" and "The Courtship of Miles Standish" are excellent history resources. The Vision Forum audio message, *How to Evaluate a Suitor*, can also be used with this section, and its review follows.

How to Evaluate a Suitor

This talk is designed for both parents and young people who anticipate the possibility of courtship and marriage. Fathers are reminded that their daughters represent the most valuable gift they will ever bestow. Emphasis is placed on the young woman and her potential suitor and their compatibility in doctrine and practical life choices. Speaker Doug Phillips argues that although a perfect suitor does not exist, suitors should meet the minimum requirements set forth in Scripture.

Format: CD

Resource for: Parents and young adults

Blessed Motherhood: (*Verses of Virtue* pp.47-90)

I love being a mother! My appreciation for this incredible gift of God's grace only increases each year. The poems and prose in this section speak deeply to my mother's heart and make a precious springboard for a study on biblical motherhood and the impact of mothers throughout history. The Vision Forum resource, *Mother*, is an excellent read-aloud book to go with this section and the review follows:

Mother

Originally published in 1911, this book written by Kathleen Norris is a fictional tale of a young woman who leaves home for what she believes to be improved circumstances. Ultimately, as God changes her heart, she learns that independence and career are nothing compared to the life and legacy of a mother, as demonstrated by her own dear mother.

Format: Book

Resource for: Family (Reading level is age 12 to adult)

Femininity Defended: (*Verses of Virtue* pp. 93-12)
"Femininity Defended" focuses on how wonderful it is to be a woman,
and teaches that the distinctions between men and women are not simply
God's design, but that we are to glory in them. This section provides many
selections that are worthy of further study, including the article, "How the
Americans Understand the Equality of the Sexes," provides great material
for discussion. A study on feminism and how this anti-biblical philosophy
has impacted our present-day view of womanhood would be an excellent
assignment to coincide with this section. Other Vision Forum resources
that help to define these concepts are: *What is Biblical Femininity?* (CD),
Training Dominion-Oriented Daughters (DVD), *So Much More* (Book),
What's a Girl to Do? (CD), and *Jennie B. and the Pilot* (CD).

What is Biblical Femininity?

Join Anna Sophia and Elizabeth Botkin as they seek to define biblical
femininity using scriptural and historical examples. Desiring to make
clear that true femininity is not based on tradition, stereotypes or
romantic images from the past, these articulate young women provide
encouragement and insight into the battles to be fought by this
generation.

Format: DVD

Resource for: Family

Training Dominion-Oriented Daughters

Offering a personal glimpse into the lives of his daughters, Anna
Sophia and Elizabeth, Geoff Botkin shares how he and his wife,
Victoria, raised their daughters for dominion-oriented service for
the kingdom of God. Some of the areas discussed are: overcoming
shyness, toys, conduct, and academic priorities. Anna Sophia and
Elizabeth are the authors of the book, *So Much More,* and speak
often at the Vision Forum Ministries Father and Daughter retreats.

Format: DVD

Resource for: Parents and young women

So Much More

Written from the perspective of two Christian young ladies raised in
a home by parents committed to biblical principles of womanhood,

this book provides a thoughtful and direct exploration of the role God intends for daughters and wives. Authors and sisters Anna Sophia and Elizabeth Botkin present a clear alternative to the generally accepted view, both within and outside the Church, that women's roles are largely interchangeable with men's. Their message is that daughters who submit to the authority and protection of their fathers, as they prepare themselves to be godly wives and mothers, will be free to experience *so much more* of God's design for their lives.

Format: Book

Resource for: Parents and young women

What's a Girl to Do?

In response to the question, "What's a girl to do?," Doug Phillips offers this bold proposal: Step back from the culture and simply look at what Scripture says on the subject. He argues that daughters are all too often negatively influenced by society, friends, and even the local church with a feministic worldview. This presentation gives hope and direction for the woman of God who desires to cultivate virtue while fully exercising her gifts.

Format: CD

Resource for: Age 10 to adult

Jennie B. and the Pilot

This is a compelling account of a daughter who loved her father and was loyal to him, but nevertheless fell prey to the two primary pressures of college life, namely feminism and the push to reject the teaching of God's Word. Jennie Chancey shares her highly personalized story of wandering, followed by restoration and the honoring of her father, while highlighting the sovereign work of God in her life. The importance of a godly father-daughter relationship resonates throughout the telling of this real-life tale.

Format: CD

Resource for: Family

<u>Daughters of Destiny</u>: (*Verses of Virtue* pp.113-126)
This section reminds us that as noble women we are to be heroic, noble, and sacrificial. A study of women in the Bible is recommended with this section as selections are included regarding Esther, Sara, Hannah and Rebbecca. For a history study, Betsy Ross and Abigail Adams are recommended examples of heroic women from America's War for Independence. The poem, "The Mothers of the West," can be memorized in honor of the frontier women whose willingness to follow their husbands and build homes in the wilderness helped to forge our great nation. Supplement your studies with related Vision Forum resources, *Joyfully at Home* and *To Have and to Hold*.

Joyfully at Home

Writing of her own transformation from a young woman with a strong desire for wordly success to one with a deep appreciation for God's design for single young women to live at home, Jasmine Baucham tackles the tough questions. You will be encouraged by her transparent, heartfelt, humerous style of writing as she shares God's vision for the home as a hub of ministry and discipleship.

Format: Book

Resource for: Mothers and daughters

To Have and to Hold

Captain Ralph Percy is a well-respected citizen in the fledgling colony of Jamestown, where his skill at swordplay is very handy indeed. When Captain Percy takes a wife from the shipload of women brought from England for the purpose of providing wives for the colonists, he unwittingly enters a world of secrets, treachery, and court intrigue. Commanded to give up his wife to the king's favorite courtier, he refuses. Filled with action, and suspense, *To Have and to Hold* weaves its thrilling tale around the early beginnings of Jamestown. Will Captain Percy continue to defend the woman who does not seem to love him? Will he obey God's Law instead of the King's, even when all fall away from his side? Your young adults will not want to put down this book written by Mary Johnston until they find out the answers!

Format: Book

Resource for: Age 12 to adult

The Blessing of Children

One of the greatest battles of our generation is to defend the blessing of children. Understanding the biomedical questions regarding the beginning and ending of life, and being prepared to approach these questions from a biblical perspective, is critical if we are to prepare our children to make wise decisions about the life-and-death questions facing Christian families every day.

Each of the products listed in this section can be used to complement a biology or history study, or can serve as individual unit studies themselves.

The Bioethics and Life Collection

Defining the biblical foundations for tackling the bioethical family issues of our time, these messages explore how we can build a culture of life in the midst of the culture of death all around us. The topics are:

The Long War Against Babies, by Doug Phillip

Should We Starve Grandpa?, by Doug Phillips and panel

The Hopeful Theology of Miscarriage, by Doug Phillips

Child Training: A Biblical Template, by Kevin Swanson

Artificial Wombs, by Doug Phillips and panel

Format: DVD (5)

Resource for: Age 10 to adult (some mature themes)

Subjects: Biology, Theology

An Encouragement: *Use this collection as a multigenerational training resource in preparation for the difficult decisions and issues of our time. Can your family define what is meant by "brain dead," and is that definition biblical? Do they know when the soul leaves the body? Does your family understand what is meant by "artificial wombs" and stem cell research and how Christians should be responding to these issues? These are just a sampling of the questions presented and dealt with from a biblical perspective in this much-needed resource for Christians living in the twenty-first century!*

Topics for Composition and Discussion

The Pill: 50 Years to Change a Culture

The Blessing of Special Needs Children

Science and the Womb

A Christian Perspective on Eldercare

Further Study

Frozen Embryos

Artificial Wombs

Trans-humanism

Cloning

Eugenics

Surrogacy

Genesis 1:27-28

Additional Vision Forum Products

Suffer the Children (CD), by Kevin Swanson

S.M. Davis Family Rebuilders Library (8 CDs)

Babies, Adoption and Family Logistics (24 CDs)

Babies, Adoption and Family Logistics

In this audio album, Jim Bob Duggar, R.C. Sproul, Jr., Doug Phillips, Flip Benham, Jennie Chancey, Kevin Swanson, and others explore ways to build a culture of life through adoption, child-birth, and the joy that comes from "large family living." Some of the topics included in this set are:

> What the Bible Says about Birth Control
>
> How to Raise a Special Needs Child
>
> The Indispensable Role of Grandparents in the Life of Children
>
> How to Manage a Large Family

Format: CD

Resource for: Age 10 to adult (some mature themes)

Subjects: Biology, Theology

An Encouragement: Do your children understand why you believe children are a blessing? Do they know how to transform the culture? Are they prepared to take a stand against our modern medical culture of death? These messages lay out before us the issues that our families will need to deal with in the twenty-first century.

Additional Vision Forum Resources

> *The Bioethics and Life Collection* (5 DVDs)
>
> *Children and the Dominion Mandate* (CD), by William O. Einwechter
>
> *Be Fruitful and Multiply* (book), by Nancy Campbell
>
> *The Role of Grandfathers in the Local Church* (CD), by Doug Phillips

Children and the Dominion Mandate

An important resource! Many professing Christians today feel that the Genesis dominion mandate does not apply in the twenty-first century, having bought into the world's false premises of overpopulation and that children are a burden. Speaker William Einwechter argues that this critical, biblical command still applies, refuting the overpopulation myth and discussing the amazing possibilities that can be realized if Christians return to obeying God's Word and begin having larger families. One of the highlights of this message is the understanding of how the dominion mandate is in essence the "after the fall" command of the great commission.

Format: CD

Resource for: Family

Subjects: Creation Science, Theology, Language Arts

An Encouragement: Not only is this message an excellent treatise on the dominion mandate, providing scriptural support and scientific research to share with your children, it can also be used to demonstrate the careful, clear exposition of Scripture. Use this audio presentation to teach your children how to make a point, and then how to defend this point with Scripture. An excellent resource for practicing note-taking and outlining skills.

Additional Vision Forum Resources

Be Fruitful and Multiply (book), by Nancy Campbell

Back to Genesis: In the Beginning , God (9 CDs)

Be Fruitful and Multiply

Searching the Scriptures, Nancy Campbell has compiled a study in book form relating God's purposes for marriage and family. With questions at the end of each chapter and a multitude of Scripture references, this book can be used as a teaching tool and as encouragement for those desiring a better foundation in the area of the blessing of children.

Format: Book

Resource for: Parents and young adults

Subjects: Biology, Home Economics

An Encouragement: This book can be studied by husband and wife and will provide a biblical perspective on the blessing of children. It also makes a wonderful study for mothers and daughters to do together.

A Culture of Virtuous Boyhood & Girlhood

Boyhood and girlhood are God-given life stages and roles, established by Him to serve His purposes. As we seek to rebuild a culture of virtue for our children, we remember that materials and resources that encourage self-discipline and a knowledge of God through the Scriptures will be an aid to us in this quest.

The following resources can be used to enhance any character study for young men.

Rebuilding a Culture of Virtuous Boyhood

There is a sacred window of time in a boy's life when he can reenact the great deeds of the past and aspire to even greater actions in the future. If properly protected by parents, boys have a level of virtuous innocence which is beautiful to behold. Although boys must be trained to become men, there is also a time when they *should* dream big dreams, undefiled by the impurities of our modern culture. In this talk, Doug Phillips presents three points directed to different phases in a boy's life: play, preparation and perseverance.

Format: CD

Resource for: Fathers and sons

An Encouragement: Why not take an hour or so as father and son to listen to this message? Fathers will come away with a better understanding of the vision their children need, and sons will be encouraged to remain faithful in their duties. Have you given thought to the toys, books, and media that your boys are using? Consider taking time to define what it means to be a young man of honor by focusing on the following resources through discussion and practical application.

Additional Vision Forum Resources

Missionary Patriarch (book), by John G. Paton

Thoughts for Young Men (book), by J.C. Ryle

Missionary Patriarch

John G. Paton served for decades among the South Sea cannibals as a faithful evangelist for Jesus Christ. This autobiographical account is a fascinating and touching history of his life from birth to the year 1897 (he died ten years later). The scene so beautifully described, where John parts from his father to go on to do his life work, is a testimony to the father-son relationship. John G. Paton's dedication and sacrifice for the cause of Christ is an amazing example to boys and girls today who, although they may never travel overseas to spread the gospel among foreign nations, *can* apply the lessons he learned to their own lives at home.

Format: Book

Resource for: Family (Reading level is 12 to adult)

Subjects: World History, Geography

An Encouragement: Read together as a family and be amazed at the providential hand of God in the life of John G. Paton. Trace the included map of the New Hebrides, the location of Paton's service, and have a short geography lesson with your children. Locate the islands on a globe or world map, and research some of the geological and climatic features on the Internet or in an encyclopedia.

Additional Vision Forum Resources

The Adventure of Missionary Heroism (book), by John C. Lambert

Thoughts for Young Men

J. C. Ryle wrote dozens of books and tracts during the 1800s about spiritual matters, among which was *Thoughts for Young Men*. This book, even though it was written over a century ago, is still unbelievably applicable today. The challenges that young men face have not changed; Satan still recognizes the unique possibilities presented by the tendencies in young men to pride, the love of pleasure, thoughtlessness, and the contempt of Christianity. Ryle's book is not long, but the truths contained are priceless and presented in a well-organized and easily understandable format.

The five chapters contained in *Thoughts for Young Men* are:

Reasons for Exhorting Young Men

Dangers to Young Men

General Counsel to Young Men

Special Rules for Young Men

Conclusion

Format: Book

Resource for: Young men (Reading level is 12 to adult)

Subjects: Language Arts

An Encouragement: In my opinion, Thoughts for Young Men *should be required reading for young men in any Christian family. To understand more about J. C. Ryle's perspective, do some research through the library or Internet and find articles about his life and works.*

Additional Vision Forum Resources

Rebuilding a Culture of Virtuous Boyhood (CD), by Doug Phillips

Bible Lessons for Manhood

Scott Brown has a heart for discipling young men. Taking biblical lessons about manhood learned from his father and other men who fought in the battlefields of World War II, Mr. Brown targets specific areas that need to be taught by father to son. Topics of discussion include:

Don't Waste Your Youth

How Fathers Prepare Their Sons for Effective Work

Don't Prejudge Disasters, and Trust in the Sovereignty of God

Lead Courageously and Build Long and Loyal Friendships

Format: CD (6)

Resource for: Fathers and sons

Subjects: History

Just as we need to defend the faith by rebuilding a culture of virtuous boyhood, so must we also rebuild a culture of virtuous girlhood. Establishing the patterns for godly womanhood in girls at a young age will provide blessings for the years to come. The following audio selections were recorded during several Father and Daughter retreats sponsored by Vision Forum Ministries. Stressing biblical femininity and the beauty of the relationship between fathers and daughters, each of these resources offers support and encouragement for dads and their girls.

True Beauty: Cultivating Christ-Centered Father-Daughter Relationships

Speakers Doug Phillips, Scott Brown, Geoff Botkin, and Anna Sophia and Elizabeth Botkin use the Scriptures to speak to the relationship between father and daughter. Topics include:

Foundational Vision for Fathers and Daughters

The Proverbs 31 Woman

Transitions from Beautiful Girlhood to Noble Womanhood

How to Prepare a Daughter for Marriage

Format: CD (8)

Resource for: Fathers and daughters

Strength & Dignity for Daughters

These two messages for young ladies given by sisters Anna Sofia and Elizabeth Botkin, daughters of Geoff Botkin, provide conceptual as well as practical ways daughters can honor and serve their fathers while functioning within the family unit. The Botkin young women share some of their own struggles as daughters, as well as their appreciation for their father, who has encouraged and directed them to aspire to biblical womanhood.

Format: CD

Resource for: Age 10 to adult

Fathers & Daughters: Why Every Father is Leaving a Legacy

Daughters are tremendously impacted by the legacy of their fathers, whether for good or bad. The primary tenet of this stirring message by Dr. Voddie Baucham is that fathers must be proactive in providing for and protecting their daughters and in setting a model for true biblical headship. Dr. Baucham vividly describes the problems that result when fathers are ignorant of and indifferent toward their duties concerning daughters.

Format: CD

Resource for: Ate 10 to adult

The Journey of Daughterhood

Using Psalm 128, Doug Phillips exhorts fathers to cultivate a special relationship with their daughters by giving them a vision of faithfulness and victory as they become women of the next generation. An excellent resource for fathers and daughters to enjoy together.

Format: CD

Resource for: Age 10 to adult

Victory for Daughters

Sisters, Sarah, Rebekah, and Hannah Zes, and Kelly Bradrick (née Brown), share about their journeys to biblical womanhood and exhort and encourage other young women to embrace this vision and give their hearts to their fathers.

Format: CD

Resource for: Age 10 to adult

Sleeping Beauty and the Five Questions

The importance of father-daughter relationships is thoughtfully described by Doug Phillips in this allegory about a king and his princess daughter, followed by some very direct and challenging remarks. This message will inspire both fathers and daughters to reevaluate the dynamics of their relationship from a spiritual perspective in contrast to the hands-off, feministic approach which pulsates through the fabric of our society, including the modern Church. The lasting lesson is that if our daughters' deep questions are not answered by their fathers, they will turn to other sources for their answers.

Format: CD

Resource for: Age 10 to adult

The Bible, the very word of God, is the foundation of all virtue and should be the basis of all learning. It is God's plan that we be able to read and understand the Scriptures. Reading instruction in our home was based on the learning of the phonetic structure of the English language. Along with this mode of teaching, however, was the use of a large-print King James Bible. The essence of all our home education was the knowledge that all of life was to be focused on the truths of the Scripture. Because of this, as soon as our children could identify a few sight words, we would start our instruction in the Book of Genesis and together we would "read" the words with the new reader pointing to and saying the words they recognized. It was a delightful time for the new reader; being able to read this precious Book was their joy!

We also exposed our children to good literature—books that would demonstrate godly character, teach providential history, and provide a biblical worldview. Several literature resources from Vision Forum were a big part of our reading journey, including the G.A. Henty series.

To this day, G.A. Henty's riveting historical novels bring back memories of my husband's voice reading to our children each night before bed!

G.A. Henty Historical Fiction Series

G.A. Henty was a soldier and war correspondent. He was rewarded for bravery during the Crimean conflict with the Turkish Order of Medjidie, Third Class. But this is not why men remember him. They remember him because of his books; over one hundred soundly researched and delightfully interesting novels. Because of Henty's many adventures around the globe, he was able to write convincing stories that transport readers to the scene of the action, involving them in the plot's twists and turns. Perhaps that is why today, more than a century after his death, boys all around the world count him high in the ranks of their favorite authors. Vision Forum sells more than 70 of Henty's classic tales.

Historian and Henty expert William Potter has written *The Boy's Guide to the Historical Adventures of G.A. Henty*, an invaluable resource for parents. Covering over seventy of Henty's most famous novels, Mr. Potter gives a brief overview of both the plot and historical context of each book, listing them by date and era. Included below is a sample of the dates and books.

Ancient History

1250 B.C. *The Cat of Bubastes*

200 B.C. *The Young Carthaginian*

A.D. 61 *Beric the Briton*

A.D. 70 *For the Temple*

The Middle Ages

870   *The Dragon and the Raven*

1066   *Wulf the Saxon*

1190   *Winning His Spurs*

1314   *In Freedom's Cause*

1340   *St. George for England*

1380   *The Lion of St. Mark*

1400   *Both Sides of the Border*

1415   *At Agincourt*

1480   *A Knight of the White Cross*

Reformation and Exploration

1519   *By Right of Conquest*

1570   *St. Bartholomew's Eve*

1579   *By Pike and Dyke*

1580   *Under Drake's Flag*

1588   *By England's Aid*

Wars of Religion and Succession

1630   *The Lion of the North*

1640   *Won by the Sword*

1650	*Friends though Divided*
1666	*When London Burned*
1669	*In the Hands of the Malays*
1680	*John Hawke's Fortune*
1690	*Orange and Green*
1700	*A Jacobite Exile*
1705	*The Bravest of the Brave*
1710	*The Cornet of Horse*
1710	*In the Irish Brigade*
1745	*Bonnie Prince Charlie*

Colonial Disruptions and Competition

1759	*With Wolfe in Canada*
1760	*With Fredrick the Great*
1776	*True to the Old Flag*
1780	*Held Fast for England*
1785	*Colonel Thorndyke's Secret*
1786	*With Clive in India*

The Napoleonic Era

1793	*In the Reign of Terror*
1795	*By Conduct and Courage*
1795	*No Surrender*
1795	*The Tiger of Mysore*
1798	*At Aboukir and Acre*
1800	*At the Point of the Bayonet*
1800	*Condemned as a Nihilist*
1807	*Through the Fray*
1810	*The Young Buglers*
1810	*Under Wellington's Command*
1812	*Through Russian Snows*
1815	*One of the 28th*

Indian Troubles and Neighbors' Wars

1820	*With Cochrane the Dauntless*
1820	*In Greek Waters*
1824	*On the Irrawaddy*
1832	*In the Hands of the Cave Dwellers*
1833	*The Treasure of the Incas*
1835	*With the British Legion*
1840	*To Herat and Cabul*

The Victorian Era

1850	*Through the Sikh War*
1850	*Redskin and Cowboy*
1850	*Dorothy's Double*
1851	*Out on the Pampas*
1854	*Jack Archer*
1856	*In Times of Peril*
1861	*With Lee in Virginia*
1861	*In the Heart of the Rockies*
1860	*The Plague Ship*
1865	*A Final Reckoning*
1865	*Out with Garibaldi*
1867	*The March to Magdala*
1870	*Maori and Settler*
1870	*The Young Franc-Tireurs*
1873	*By Sheer Pluck*
1873	*The March to Coomasie*
1878	*For Name and Fame*
1880	*The Young Colonists*
1880	*A Chapter of Adventures*
1885	*The Dash for Khartoum*
1888	*Sturdy and Strong*

1896	*Through Three Campaigns*
1898	*With Kitchner in the Soudan*
1899	*With Buller in Natal*
1900	*With the Allies to Pekin*
1900	*With Roberts to Pretoria*

One of my son's personal Henty favorites is *Beric the Briton: A Story of the Roman Invasion*. Beric is the young chieftain of a small tribe in Briton, under Roman occupation. He joins an attempt by the maltreated Queen Boadicia to throw the Romans into the sea and is soon involved in a succession of bloody battles. Defeated by the better trained legionaries, he seeks refuge in a swamp and harries the enemy for many months until finally surrounded and captured. Carried to Rome as a gladiator, Beric is put to severe training, but before he can enter the ring as a warrior he chooses to defend a Christian girl from a lion - with no weapon but a cloak. His success draws the attention of Emperor Nero, a "generous" but fickle friend. At last, Beric is forced to make a decision; whether to continue a life of dangerous ease in Nero's palace, or protect his betrothed and become a hunted outlaw. The decision made by this young man will have a profound impact on the people of Britain!

Format: Book

Resource for: Age 10 to adult (Reading level is age 12 to adult)

Subjects: Literature, History, Geography, Language Arts

An Encouragement: Not only do Henty books provide hours of enjoyment through personal or listen-along reading, but they can make the foundation for an awesome history curriculum as well! Why not purchase Vision Forum's complete Henty collection, and using the Boy's Guide to the Historical Adventures of G.A. Henty, *have your children begin the process of learning world history through the eyes of adventure? My husband, who was a history major in college, says he learned almost as much history reading these books as he did in his college courses. Try having your history buff design a curriculum based upon each Henty adventure that includes a further study of the times, geography and of course demonstrating God's providential hand in history.*

Ideas for Composition and Discussion

Pick one of Henty's historical characters and research and write a paper about his life and impact.

Write an article about a war covered in one of Henty's books, focusing on the reasons for the conflict.

Illustrate one of Henty's characters. Give extra points for embellishments such as weapons or armor.

Encourage a budding author by assigning the writing of a similar adventure.

Create a book jacket by writing a description of the book and illustrating the cover.

Start a bedtime tradition of reading from a Henty book together each night.

Write a paragraph describing the character traits of each Henty hero.

Additional Vision Forum Resources

R.M. Ballantyne Christian Adventure Library

Providential Battles Vols. 1 & 2 (8 CDs)

Sabers, Spears, and Catapults (4 CDs)

G.A. Henty and R.M. Ballantyne have many similarities, but they wrote about different subjects. Henty normally based his books on significant wars and events in history. Ballantyne, on the other hand, wrote largely about events in the nineteenth century, often choosing exotic geographic locations in which to center his tales. The novels of both authors are replete with pirates, natives, villains, and, of course, the upstanding young man who must defeat them all to win the day!

R.M. Ballantyne Christian Adventure Library (20 Volumes)

In the nineteenth century, the name R.M. Ballantyne was synonymous with one word: adventure. Thousands of boys read, re-read, and triple-read his books, a firm testimony to his skill as a writer. During the mid-to-late 1900s, R.M. Ballantyne's formerly beloved works faded in popularity, probably because of his unabashedly Christian message. Today, however, the young people of America can renew their acquaintance with this wholesome author, the man whom Robert Louis Stevenson named "Ballantyne The Brave."

The Author:

R.M. Ballantyne was born in Scotland in 1825, and was the nephew of James Ballantyne, the editor and publisher of poet and novelist Sir Walter Scott. Although exposed to great literature from a very young age, Ballantyne did not begin writing seriously until after a six-year stay in the wilderness of North America, where he worked for the Hudson's Bay Company. After his first few books, publishers began to notice

Ballantyne's skill with words, and his path to fame was begun, although many bumps still lay ahead. He did not marry until the age of forty, by which time his name was already known far and wide. Ballantyne died in Rome from a rare sickness called Meniere's Disease, after writing over 100 books and exerting a profound influence upon generations of boys.

The Books:

There is no set sequence in which to read Ballantyne's books, excepting *The Coral Island* and *The Gorilla Hunters*, which are to be read in that order. The majority of his main characters are young men who are placed in challenging situations where they learn to serve God and follow His principles, while involved in breath-taking adventures. Ballantyne researched his books extensively, often traveling to the locales in which they were set. For example, when writing *Fighting the Flames* he rode to several fires on a London fire-truck, and actually earned a medal for bravery, *The Young Fur Traders* was based on his time in the wintry wilds of Canada and his research for *The Pirate City* led him disguised as a Muslim into the Arab quarter of Algiers!

Approximate times and places:

<u>Title</u>	<u>Time</u>	<u>Setting</u>
The Norsemen in the West	c. 1000	North America
Hunted and Harried	1680s	Scotland
Red Rooney	early 1700s	Arctic regions
*The Cannibal Islands**	1768-1779	Pacific Ocean
*The Pioneers**	1789	North America
The Lonely Island	1790-1829	Pitcairn Island
The Pirate City	1817	Algiers
The Dog Crusoe	early-mid 1800s	North America
Ungava	early-mid 1800s	North America
The Young Fur Traders	early-mid 1800s	Canada
Fighting the Flames	1861	London
Deep Down	c. 1868	Cornwall
Post Haste	c. 1880	London
Blue Lights	1880s	Soudan
The Gorilla Hunters	mid-late 1800s	Africa
The Coral Island	mid-late 1800s	South Sea Island
*Fast in the Ice**	1800s	Arctic regions

The Island Queen	1800s	South Sea Island
Gascoyne	1800s	South Sea Island
*Fighting the Whales**	1800s	Atlantic Ocean
The Giant of the North	1800s	Arctic regions
Martin Rattler	1800s	South America

*Books marked with an asterisk are included with other novels in the R.M. Ballantyne Series.

Format: Book

Resource for: Age 10 to adult (Reading level is age 12 to adult)

Subjects: Literature, History, Geography, Language Arts

These books are excellent for studying particular time periods or geographical locations, at the same time instilling in young people a love for God and a firm understanding of right and wrong.

Additional Vision Forum Resources

G.A. Henty Historical Fiction Series, by G.A. Henty

BallantyneTheBrave.com

Young ladies have also been known to enjoy the reading of books by Henty and Ballantyne. However, Vision Forum has reprinted a series specifically directed toward encouraging virtuous girlhood; *The Elsie Dinsmore Library*.

The Elsie Dinsmore Library

Girls of all ages have loved the sweet beauty and trusting faith of Elsie Dinsmore as she struggles against a harsh and unloving world. She has become a model for generations of young ladies who sympathize and rejoice with her as she travels through life's vicissitudes. Elsie has a passion for Christ, and a meek and quiet spirit, but she will not violate her principles, regardless of what the reward or punishment may be. This delightful series was written by Martha Finley, a Christian author in the 1800s, who wanted to inspire girls to follow God and live according to his commandments.

Elsie Dinsmore (Vol. 1)

Elsie's Holiday (Vol. 2)

Elsie's Girlhood (Vol. 3)

Elsie's Womanhood (Vol. 4)

Elsie's Motherhood (Vol. 5)

Elsie's Children (Vol. 6)

Elsie's Widowhood (Vol. 7)

Grandmother Elsie (Vol. 8)

Elsie's New Relations (Vol. 9)

Elsie at Nantucket (Vol. 10)

The Two Elsies (Vol. 11)

Elsie's Kith and Kin (Vol. 12)

Format: Books

Resource for: Age 10 to adult

Subjects: Literature, History, Language Arts

Topics for Composition and Discussion

How does the Elsie series teach biblical truths and inspire feminine behavior?

Elsie Dinsmore: A Woman of Principle

Life in the 1800s and the Civil War

This is another series which can be used to read aloud to your family. As reprints from another era, these books would not be considered "politically correct."

Additional Vision Forum Resources

Elsie Dinsmore Vol. 1 (8 CDs)

Elsie's Holiday Vol. 2 (9 CDs)

Elsie's Girlhood Vol. 3 (8 CDs)

Two other literature resources to encourage virtue in the lives of boys and girls are:

The Princess Adelina

Eighth-century Germany is stirred to its depths when a pagan prince falls in love with a Christian maiden and she is forced to become his bride. Although he is disposed to be lenient to Christians because of his wife's faith, the prince's mother wants nothing to do with these Christians—and she will do anything to destroy them. Based on a true story, thus begins this tale of heroism and bravery, not by sword-wielding warriors, but by a frightened young girl torn between her love for Christ and her husband. Slandered, persecuted, exiled, she remains firm, even when there appears to be no hope. The Princess Adelina shows that bravery is not measured by the strength of the arm, but by the power of the will.

Format: Book

Resource for: Age 12 to adult

Subject: Literature, History

An Encouragement: This book makes a wonderful read-aloud to your children. Modeled in some ways after the biblical story of Esther, the making of difficult choices and the cost of living out your faith can be discussed. An excellent precursor to a study of Christian princesses and how their lives have impacted history down through the ages.

The Adventure of Missionary Heroism

What better occasion for bravery can be presented than when exercised in spreading the Holy Word of God? *The Adventure of Missionary Heroism* may read like a work of fiction, but it's not. Each incredible story is a true recounting of the struggles and sacrifices by men and women such as Dr. Chamberlain, Alexander Mackay, or Stephen and Mary Riggs and Princess Kapiolani. They faced overwhelming difficulties, including crocodiles, tigers, elephants, and snakes (not to mention cannibals). This book will motivate readers to dig deeper into the lives of these Christian heroes, and can be used as a tool for unit studies about missionary endeavors.

Format: Book

Resource for: Family (Reading level is age 12 to adult)

Subjects: Literature, History

An Encouragement: This is one of my favorite read-aloud books! Filled with stories of men and women with a passion for the Lord Jesus Christ who lived lives of adventure and sacrifice, it may lead some young people to consider missionary service for themselves. Why not assign your student a geography study, and additional research, on the areas of Asia, America, Africa and the South Pacific where most of the book's action takes place?

Additional Vision Forum Resources:

Missionary Patriarch (book), by John G. Paton

History of the World: A.D. (20 CDs)

#15: "Nineteenth Century Missions," by William Potter

The New England Primer

Originally published in 1690, and used to teach most of the Founding Fathers of our country to read and write, this volume is thought to be one of the most influential Christian textbooks in history. Combining the study of the Bible with alphabet, vocabulary, prose, and poetry, this reprinted book also includes the Shorter Catechism.

Format: Book

Resource for: Age 5 to adult

Subjects: Reading, Language Arts, History

The Original Blue Back Speller

Actually used by Benjamin Franklin to teach his granddaughter to read and spell, and originally written in 1783, this reprinted book contains a concise overview of the phonetic method of teaching reading. The *Speller* can be used as a resource of examples of word families and the teaching of syllabication.

Format: Book

Resource for: Age 5 to adult

Subjects: Reading, Language Arts, History

An Encouragement: Because these patriotic textbooks are reprinted from an older versions, spelling and the clarity of print may frustrate younger children. I would personally use these as a resource and make my own "charts" for reading instruction and practice. The word lists can also be used for spelling, vocabulary enrichment, and handwriting. Excellent passages are included for virtuous memorization.

These books are a must-have when teaching colonial American History. What rich insight can be gathered about our Founding Fathers in the study of the stories, catechism, and poetry that they also studied!

The Development of the History of Christianity and Western Civilization

W e need to teach our children to defend their faith by understanding God's providential hand in history. I know of no better way to do this than to expose them to men who have a passionate love and appreciation for God and for the subject they teach. The following Vision Forum products not only help us to see the "how and why" of God's work in history, but also where our families fit into His marvelous plan.

The History of Christianity and Western Civilization Study Course

This work emanates from the *piece de resistance* of all the Faith & Freedom Tours presented by Vision Forum Ministries to date. Designed to cover over two thousand years of Christianity and Western Civilization, it was recorded and filmed at multiple European locations of historic significance. Its focus is on God's providential provision for His Church since its inception in the face of powerful adversaries and sometimes overwhelming opposition. Highlights include talks from the Catacombs and the Coliseum in Rome, messages from Calvin's Geneva, and treatments of the Covenanters in Scotland and the Pilgrims of England's Scrooby Manner. Other locations include Paris and Pompei.

The student of Church history will particularly appreciate the treatment of distinctions between Roman Catholicism and Reformation Christianity. One fascinating aspect deals with the contrast of architectural messages demonstrated by Catholic cathedrals versus Reformed Church buildings. The speakers also trace the impact of ancient Rome on Christianity and Western Civilization. They deal not only with the importance of Roman roads, law, and language, but also Roman concepts and ways of thinking which have infiltrated the Christian Church down to the present day.

These lectures are presented by Doug Phillips, pastor and Church historian Dr. Joseph Morecraft III, historian William Potter, and architectural expert and filmmaker Colin Gunn.

The course consists of a Study Guide, a 9-hour DVD Set, and 50+ MP3 audio lectures.

Resource for: Ages 12 to adult

Subjects: World History, Theology, Fine Arts

Western Civilization Collection

Not to be confused with the previously-described course of study, this powerful collection includes two DVD sets, both featuring ten DVDs, and was filmed in Boston at the Reformation 500 Celebration.

Christianity & Western Civilization

John Calvin was born into a volatile time full of conflict between the traditional Catholic church and a new breed of thinkers, called Protestants (also known as Huguenots in France). It was the Reformation, a time when men reexamined the Bible and challenged the enormous heresies of the Catholic church, only to be called heretics themselves and sent to burn at the stake. The Reformation affected all areas of culture and orthodoxy, paving the way for religious liberty in Europe and the New World. Each of the ten DVDs in this box set holds a powerful message from scholars and historians who have studied the Reformation's impact on Christianity and Western Civilization, exploring subjects ranging from Calvin's involvement in the Geneva Bible to the use of biblical law in the American colonies.

Format: DVD (10)

Resource for: Ages 10 to adult

Subjects: History, Theology, Language Arts, Music

An Encouragement: *Viewing these ten DVDs made me understand without a doubt the value of teaching history in conjunction with theology. Each DVD stands alone as a unique message on the providential hand of God in history. An excellent project for independent study, I also highly recommend families to watch these together as a part of your history curriculum. Used in conjunction with the other Vision Forum history resources, or more traditional textbooks, if that is your preference, or even as a stand-alone unit study, the truths and insights presented by these men are life-changing.*

DVD Highlights:

DVD #1: Five Hundred Years of Liberty Birthed by the Reformation

Doug Phillips provides a panoramic overview of the Reformation while introducing the audience to the worldview issues articulated by John Calvin, and demonstrates how Calvin helped to lay the foundations of freedom for modern Western Civilization.

Topics for Composition and Discussion

>   Calvin's Impact on the Family

>   The Origination of Representative Government

>   What is the greatest battle of our day?

>   How did the reformation lay the foundation of freedom for modern Western Civilization?

Further Study

>   Council of Nicea

>   Geneva Psalter

>   Gregorian Chant

>   Five *Solas* of the Faith

>   Doctrine of Providence

Additional Vision Forum Resources

>   *Reformation and Revival* (book), by John Brown

Reformers and Revolutionaries (10 DVDs):

> #1: "In Defense of the *Solas* of the Reformation," by Dr. Joseph Morecraft III

History of the World: A.D. (20 CDs):

> #5, 6: "How Augustine Changed the World" Pts. 1 & 2, by Dr. Joseph Morecraft III

> #9: "What Every Christian Needs to Know about the Reformation," by Dr. Joseph Morecraft III

A Comprehensive Defense of the Providence of God (21 DVDs):

> #2: "The Providential Beginnings of America," by Dr. Paul Jehle

DVD #2: The Man of the Millennium

Dr. Morecraft shares how John Calvin is arguably the most important man of the past 1,000 years, and how his influence has reached into the twenty-first century.

Topics for Composition and Discussion

Two Marks of a True Church

Calvin and Evangelism

Calvinism and the Twenty-First Century

Further Study

Libertines

Anabaptists

Antinomianism

Alexander Duff

Additional Vision Forum Resources

John Calvin: Man of the Millennium (book), by Philip Vollmer

Reformers & Revolutionaries (10 DVDs):

> #3: "John Calvin's View of Law," by Dr. Joseph Morecraft III

> #8: "Calvin's Doctrine of Worship," by Dr. Joseph Morecraft III

History of the World: A.D (20 CDs):

> #10: "The Global Influence of John Calvin," by Dr. Joseph Morecraft III

DVD #3: From Terror to Triumph: The Victory of the Church through Perilous Times

Dr. Foster traces the victory of the church from ancient Rome to the American Revolution, offering encouragement and insight into our place in present-day history. This lecture is an excellent foundation for a study of colonial American History.

Ideas and Topics for Composition and Discussion

Why do we need the lessons of history?

How is God using home educators in history?

Name and describe the five evils found in ancient civilizations.

Compare and contrast the French and American Revolutions.

Further Study

Plymouth Plantation

St. Bartholomew's Day

Twelve Terrors of France

Additional Vision Forum Resources

History of the World (10 DVDs):

  #9: "The Miracle of America," by Dr. Marshall Foster

History of the World: A.D. (20 CDs):

  #2: "A Brief History of Martyrdom, Persecution and Inquisitions," by Dr. Joseph Morecraft III

  #11: "The History of the English Church," by Dr. Joseph Morecraft III

Landmarks and Liberty: The New England Faith & Freedom Tour (1 MP3 or 8 CDs)

Beric the Briton (book), by G.A. Henty

St. Bartholomew's Day (book), by G.A. Henty

Of Plymouth Plantation (book), by William Bradford

DVD #4: The Bible Unleashed: Calvin's Role in Producing the Geneva Bible

Dr. Foster demonstrates how the sixteenth century was the most transformational of centuries since the birth of Christ as he describes how the world was changed by the Word of God being made available to all people.

Topics for Composition and Discussion

The Bible: Weapon for Changing History

The Power of the Sword

Africa: A Christian Nation?

Why did the medieval Church keep the common Bible from the people?

Further Study

The Divine Right of Kings

John Hus

John Wycliff

Henry VIII

David Livingstone

Bible Translators

Additional Resources From Vision Forum

History of the World: A.D. (20 CDs):

#15: "Nineteenth Century Missions," by William Potter

Reformers & Revolutionaries (10 DVDs):

#5: "Calvin's Spiritual Forefathers," by Marcus Serven

A Comprehensive Defense of the Providence of God (21 DVDs):

#5: "The Coming of the Bible to America," by Dr. Marshall Foster

John Calvin: Man of the Millennium (book), by Philip Vollmer:

Chapter 28: "Calvin's Influence on England," by Dr. Joseph Morecraft III

Reformation & Revival (book), by John Brown:

"Appendix B," by Dr. Marshall Foster

The Adventure of Missionary Heroism (book), by John C. Lambert

DVD #5: The Influence of the Reformation on Global Exploration and Warfare

William Potter illustrates how the sixteenth and seventeenth centuries were years of tremendous global exploration through his descriptions of military strategy and warfare.

Ideas and Topics for Composition and Discussion

Compare the Battle of Derry with the building of the wall in Nehemiah.

How did the Battle of Derry influence the War for Independence?

The Boers and the Zulus

The Rise of the Dutch Republic

Further Study

Dutch East India Company

Dutch West India Company

Prince William of Orange

Ulster Plantation

Additional Vision Forum Resources

By Pike and Dyke (book), by G.A. Henty

Under Drake's Flag (book), by G.A. Henty

By England's Aid (book), by G.A. Henty

The Lion of the North (book), by G.A. Henty

Won by the Sword (book), by G.A. Henty

The Young Colonists (book), by G.A. Henty

DVD #6: The Reformation Influence on Art and Culture

In this message, Doug Phillips shares how the Reformers spearheaded a biblically-based revival of arts and music. This is an excellent introduction to any high school-level course on the arts.

Ideas and Topics for Composition and Discussion

How do music and art impact the culture?

Write about the theology of aesthetics and the Reformers.

Read Exodus 36-40 and study God's design for the Tabernacle.

Further Study

Johann Sebastian Bach

A Mighty Fortress Is Our God

Baroque Period of Music

Medieval Period of Art

Additional Vision Forum Resources

History of the World (10 DVDs):

#4: "Jerusalem & Athens: Antithesis Between Hebrew & Greek Cultures," by Doug Phillips

Mysteries of the Ancient World (12 CDs):

#1: "The Mystery of Origins: The Cosmic Implications of Creation *Ex Nihilo*," by Doug Phillips

How God Wants Us to Worship Him (book), by Dr. Joseph Morecraft III

DVD #7: Calvin and Darwin: The Impact of Friendships on Civilization

Doug Phillips shares how friendships throughout history have impacted the world for both good and evil as he highlights the legacies of John Calvin and Charles Darwin.

Topics for Composition and Discussion

David and Jonathan: How Friendship Impacts the World

A Biblical Treatise on Choosing Friends

A Legacy of Friendship: Calvin, Farrel, and Viret

Further Study

Adam Sedgwick

Martin Luther

Margaret Sanger

Additional Vision Forum Resources

The Family Table (CD), by Doug Phillips

The Centrality of the Home in Evangelism and Discipleship (CD), by Dr. Voddie Baucham

The Mysterious Islands (DVD)

Darwin vs. Calvin (DVD)

Manly Friendships (CD), by Doug Phillips

DVD #8: How Calvinism Built New England, How New England Built America

Dr. Paul Jehle traces the impact of Calvinism on the colonies of New England and the new nation of America.

Topics for Composition and Discussion

The Homeschool Movement: Impacting the Culture of the United States

What the Individual Embraces in His Mind Becomes His Conduct and Culture for the Future

Calvin and New England

Further Study

Age of Enlightenment

John Wise's Sermon of 1717

"Jeremiads"

Great Awakening

Salem Witch Trial

Additional Vision Forum Resources

Pilgrims vs. Indians (CD), by Dougs Phillips

Puritans vs. Witches (CD), by Dr. Paul Jehle

Reformers & Revolutionaries (10 DVDs):

#3: "John Calvin's View of Law," by Dr. Joseph Morecraft III

Landmarks and Liberty: The New England Faith & Freedom Tour (1 MP3 or 8 CDs)

The Providential Nexus of Jamestown and Plymouth (DVD), by Dr. Paul Jehle

DVD #9: Competing Views of Dominion: Roman Catholic vs. Reformed

Dan Ford presents a fascinating comparison of the dominion philosophies of those seeking to establish the New World.

Topics for Composition and Discussion

The Failure of Tyranny: The Success of Liberty

The Influence of John Calvin on the Colonization of America

Wives for Jamestown

Calvin on "The Mayflower"

Further Study

Magnalia Christi Americana

Calvin's Commentary on Isaiah

Writs of Assistance

Massachusetts' Proclamation of Independence

Additional Vision Forum Resources

History of the World: A.D (20 CDs):

#19, 20: "The Twentieth Century : A Theological and Historical Autopsy, Pts. 1 & 2"

To Have and to Hold (book), by Mary Johnston

A Comprehensive Defense of the Providence of God in the Founding of America (21 DVDs)

The Bible Lessons of John Quincy Adams for His Son (book), edited by Doug Phillips

You May Not Take Our Guns (DVD), by Larry Pratt

Patriots vs. Tories (CD), by Joseph Morecraft III

By Right of Conquest (book), by G.A. Henty

From Jamestown to Jubilee: The Virginia Faith & Freedom Tour (1 MP3 or 9 CDs)

Line in the Sand: The Texas Faith & Freedom Tour (MP3)

DVD #10: The Use of Biblical Law in the American Colonies

Col. John Eidsmoe shows the impact of biblical law in the colonies, revealing the foundation it laid for the American constitutional republic to come.

Topics for Composition and Discussion

The Biblical Law for Kings

Israel: The First Example of Separation of Church and State

Christian Conscience and Natural Law

Further Study

Jonathan Edwards

Ten Commandments

John Roche

John Winthrop

Roger Williams

Theocracy

Additional Vision Forum Resources

History of the World: A.D. (20 CDs):

#13, 14: "The History of the Law of Nations," Pts. 1 & 2, by Dr. Paul Jehle

#3: "The Christian History of the Common Law," by Doug Phillips

The New England Primer

From Jamestown to Jubilee: The Virginia Faith & Freedom Tour (1 MP3 or 9 CDs)

Landmarks and Liberty: The New England Faith & Freedom Tour (1 MP3 or 9 CDs)

The Original Blue Back Speller

The Best of the Witherspoon School of Law and Public Policy, (16 CDs)

Reformers & Revolutionaries (10 DVDs)

Reformers & Revolutionaries explores the faithful work and lives of Christians who stood fast under unimaginable persecution. From the Waldenses in Italy to Martin Luther in Germany, and from Calvin's doctrines of worship and family life to John Knox's vigorous defense of the Church in Scotland, these powerful lectures provide unique insights into the lives and actions of great Christians and give hope to modern families attempting to stem the tide of spiritual degeneration in our own culture.

Resource for: Age 10 to adult

Subjects: History, Theology, Language Arts

An Encouragement: The Reformers & Revolutionaries *DVD set is an excellent complement to the Christianity and Western Civilization DVD set previously described. Both collections can also be used as a foundation for a unit study by incorporating music, art, and the science of the Reformation time period into your study. Of course, any study of this time period can be applied toward meeting your students' world history requirements. Although the DVDs focus on the lives and messages of Martin Luther, John Calvin, and John Knox, the timeline on the slipcase is a wonderful resource for identifying other key Reformers whose lives can be studied and researched as well. Why not encourage a family reenacting night with members researching, and then sharing by written word or drama, about the life of "their" Reformer? Clothing of the time can also be researched, and making period costumes would further enhance the experience of this study.*

Following are two highlighted DVDs from this set.

DVD #9: The Reformers and the Paper Trail of Freedom

Dr. Marshall Foster traces historical documents through history, explaining how the Declaration of Independence was impacted by ancient papers such as the Magna Charta, and is foundational to our understanding of American history.

Additional Vision Forum Products

The Providential Nexus of Plymouth and Jamestown (DVD), by Dr. Paul Jehle

From Jamestown to Jubilee: The Virginia Faith & Freedom Tour (1 MP3 or 9 CDs)

A Comprehensive Defense of the Providence of God (21 DVDs):

#6: "The Literature of Freedom of Our Founding Fathers," by Dan Ford

DVD #7: John Calvin on the Biblical Doctrine of the Family

Drawing from Calvin's counsel on family life, Scott Brown summarizes Calvin's contribution to the biblical doctrine of the family.

Additional Vision Forum Resources

How to Disciple Your Family (10 DVDs)

Building a Family That Will Stand (7 CDs)

The Master's Plan for Fathers (7 CDs)

Give Me Your Heart, My Son (8 CDs)

History of the World (10 DVDs):

#10: "How Families Have Changed the World," by Dr. Marshall

Foster

How the Scots Saved Christendom (12 CDs)

The Reformation 500 Celebration

This 2-part audio album contains 37 CDs and 2 MP3 CDs, and highlights the impact of the Reformation on the Western World. An audio combination of the *Christianity & Western Civilization* DVD set and *Reformers & Revolutionaries* DVD set plus additional recordings, this audio album can stand alone or be used in conjunction with those DVDs. There will be some overlap of sessions.

Reformation & Revival: The Story of the English Puritans

Defining as Puritanism the historical movement which took place in English history from Queen Elizabeth's ascension to the throne in 1558 to the death of Oliver Cromwell in 1658, and providing an excellent survey of the struggle for religious liberty during that time, this book can be used in conjunction with the *Christianity & Western Civilization* and *Reformers & Revolutionaries* DVD series. A succinct overview of the origin, triumphs, and downfall of Puritanism, *Reformation & Revival*, originally written by John Brown and featuring additional commentary by Dr. Joseph Morecraft III and Dr. Marshall Foster, can also be used as a study by itself. The appendices listed below provide tremendous insight into the men and issues of the Puritan time period.

Appendix A: "Oliver Cromwell: Lord Protector of England, Scotland, and Ireland"

Appendix B: "The History and Impact of the Geneva Bible"

Appendix C: "The Solemn League and Covenant"

Appendix D: "Act of Supremacy"

Appendix E: "Elizabeth's Act of Uniformity (1559)"

Appendix F: "The Conventicle Act of 1593"

Appendix G: "The Millenary Petition (1603)"

Appendix H: "Historical Timeline"

Format: Book

Resource for: Age 12 to adult (Reading level is age 14 to adult)

Subjects: World History, U.S. History, American Government

This book provides an excellent framework for any study necessitating an understanding of the Puritan movement and its impact on history.

Additional Vision Forum Resources

History of the World: A.D. (20 CDs):

#9: "What Every Christian Needs to Know About the Reformation," by Dr. Joseph Morecraft III

#12: "The Remarkable Life Of Oliver Cromwell," by Dr. Joseph Morecraft III

John Calvin: Man of the Millennium

Perfect as a family read-aloud biography or as a source of information for the independent student of Reformation and American history, this book, originally written by Phillip Volmer, provides a clear and concise overview of the life of John Calvin. The additional chapters written by Dr. Morecraft and Dr. Good on Calvin's influence on Holland, Scotland and America, are an incredible asset to anyone seeking to understand the influence and impact of the life and writings of John Calvin on the world, and particularly the founding of America.

Format: Book

Resource for: Age 10 to adult (Reading level is ages 12 to adult)

Subjects: World History, U. S. History, Literature

An Encouragement: *If you are interested in making sure your family understands the amazing heritage that is ours because of the sacrifice and devotion of those who have gone before us, this book provides a unique and insightful overview.*

Additional Vision Forum Resources

History of the World (10 DVDs):

#8: "America's Four Hundredth Birthday: Jamestown's Legacy of Law and Gospel," by Doug Phillips

#9: "The Miracle of America," by Dr. Marshall Foster

History of the World: A.D. (20 CDs):

#10: "The Global Influence of John Calvin," by Dr. Joseph Morecraft III

#17: "The American Republic," by Dr. Marshall Foster

Christianity & Western Civilization (10 DVDs):

> #4: "The Bible Unleashed: Calvin's Role in Producing the Geneva Bible," by Dr. Marshall Foster

> #8: "How Calvinism Built New England, How New England Built America," by Dr. Paul Jehle

Reformers & Revolutionaries (10 DVDs):

> #3: "John Calvin's View of Law," by Dr. Joseph Morecraft III

> #7: "John Calvin on the Biblical Doctrine of Family," by Scott Brown

> #8: "Calvin's Doctrine of Worship," by Dr. Joseph Morecraft III

From Jamestown to Jubilee: The Virginia Faith & Freedom Tour

Imagine a course of study that begins with the founding of Jamestown, handles the Great Awakening in Virginia, describes the importance and personages of colonial Williamsburg, and winds up with a fascinating look at the life and career of General Thomas "Stonewall" Jackson. All of this and more is to be found in *From Jamestown to Jubilee*, highlighting God's providential work in the affairs of men. Doug Phillips and historian William Potter offer glimpses into the lives and times of outstanding men of colonial Virginia, and the formative years of our country, by examining the homes in which they lived. Mount Vernon, Monticello, and Scotchtown have much to say about the priorities and perspectives of their owners, George Washington, Thomas Jefferson and Patrick Henry, respectively.

Format: 1 MP3 or 9 CDs

Resource for: Age 10 to adult

Subjects: U.S. History, Language Arts

Topics for Composition and Discussion

> Psalm 78 and the Study of History

> What is a Providential Perspective?

> The Family and the Building of America

> Jamestown: Patriotism, Piety and Perspective

> Samuel Davies and Patrick Henry

> "Stonewall" Jackson and the Virginia Military Institute

Additional Vision Forum Resources

Poems for Patriarchs (book), edited by Doug Phillips

Christians vs. Deists (CD), by Dr. Joseph Morecraft

Christ in the Camp (book), by J. William Jones

The Life and Campaigns of Stonewall Jackson (book), by Robert Lewis Dabney

George Washington: America's Joshua (CD), by Doug Phillips

History of the World (10 DVDs):

> #8: "America's 400th Birthday: Jamestown's Legacy of Law and Gospel," by Doug Phillips

History of the World: A.D. (20 CDs):

> #3: "The Christian History of the Common Law," by Doug Phillips

> #17: "The American Republic," by Dr. Marshall Foster

A Comprehensive Defense of the Providence of God in the Founding of America (21 DVDs)

The Providential Nexus of Plymouth and Jamestown

This fascinating DVD by Dr. Paul Jehle concentrates on the tensions between the two legacies of Jamestown and Plymouth. Showing how God providentially wove these elements together to form the United States of America, Dr. Jehle also provides illuminating analogies to issues we all deal with in the Christian life. An excellent resource to use as a framework for the study of the founding of our nation. Watch this on Thanksgiving Day to really appreciate all we have to be thankful for!

Format: DVD

Resource for: Age 10 to adult

Subjects: U.S. History, American Government, Language Arts

Ideas and Topics for Composition and Discussion

Compare and contrast the legacies of Jamestown and Plymouth.

Jamestown and Plymouth: A Melding of Theology

The Purpose of Separation

1619: Women for Jamestown

Additional Vision Forum Resources

To Have and To Hold (book), by Mary Johnston

Of Plymouth Plantation (book), by William Bradford

Jamestown: Ancient Landmark, Modern Battleground (DVD), by Doug Phillips

From Jamestown to Jubilee: The Virginia Faith & Freedom Tour (1 MP3 or 9 CDs)

Landmarks and Liberty: The New England Faith & Freedom Tour (1 MP3 or 8 CDs)

Of Plymouth Plantation

What better man could be found to write about Plymouth Plantation than William Bradford, one of the leaders who brought that group of determined men and women to the untamed North American shores? *Of Plymouth Plantation* was originally published in 1656, having been written as a journal between 1620 and 1646. Bradford's work is the single most complete book about the settlement, and has the amazing perspective of a man who not only was a first-hand witness, but also an important actor in the unfolding scene of the New World. This book includes the names of all those who came over in the *Mayflower,* and their subsequent history.

Format: Book

Resource for: Age 10 to adult (Reading level is age 12 to adult)

Subjects: U.S. History, World History, Language Arts

Ideas and Topics for Composition and Discussion

The Multigenerational Vision of the Pilgrims

Outline the path of the Separatist journey from England to Holland and then on the New World.

Draw a map of the area first settled by the Pilgrims.

Study the geography of the Plymouth area.

Further Study

Thanksgiving

William Bradford

John Robinson

Squanto

William Brewster

Priscilla Mullins

Miles Standish

Additional Vision Forum Resources

Verses of Virtue (book):"The Wedding of Priscilla" from *The Courtship of Miles Standish,* by Henry Wadsworth Longfellow

The Providential Nexus of Jamestown and Plymouth (DVD), by Dr. Paul Jehle

Landmarks and Liberty: The New England Faith & Freedom Tour (1 MP3 or 9 CDs)

Christianity & Western Civilization (10 DVDs):

#3: "From Terror to Triumph: The Victory of the Church through Perilous Times," by Dr. Marshall Foster

#8: "How Calvinism Built New England, How New England Built America," by Dr. Paul Jehle

#10: "The Use of Biblical Law in the Colonies," by Col. John Eidsmoe

History of the World: A.D. (20 CDs):

#10: "The Global Influence of John Calvin," by Dr. Joseph Morecraft III

#17: "The American Republic," by Dr. Marshall Foster

Jamestown: Ancient Landmark, Modern Battleground

Although originally designed as a "call" to participate in the Jamestown Quadricentennial Celebration sponsored by Vision Forum Ministries in 2007, this 38-minute DVD may be one of the most important teaching tools you can purchase for your family. Do your children understand how history is being rewritten by the scholars and historians of our day? Tracing celebrations through our nation's history of the founding of Jamestown, Doug Phillips demonstrates how careful we must be in the teaching of true, accurately documented history to our children. All ages can watch and discuss this video about how the "experts" and media representatives of our day are rewriting history based upon their own cultural presuppositions.

Format: DVD

Resource for: Family

Subjects: U. S. History, Language Arts

Ideas and Topics for Composition and Discussion

> Make application of this video by studying current news events and how the details are often misrepresented by those with an anti-family agenda.

> Design your own monument of remembrance to show honor to a family member or event of importance in your family history.

> Discuss and document the Great Commission and the founding of America.

> Research the history of Pocahontas and the impact of her descendants on America.

Additional Vision Forum Resources

> *Jamestown to Jubilee: The Virginia Faith & Freedom Tour* (1 MP3 or 9 CDs)

> *History of the World: A.D.* (20 CDs)

> *The Providential Nexus of Jamestown and Plymouth* (DVD), by Dr. Paul Jehle

> *A Comprehensive Defense of the Providence of God in the Founding of America* (21 DVDs)

A Comprehensive Defense of the Providence of God in the Founding of America

The Jamestown Quadricentennial formed the backdrop for an authentic celebration of God's providential work in American history. This collection of approximately nineteen hours of material zeroes in on the founding and significance of Jamestown, but also includes Bacon's Rebellion and George Washington. Americans will not appreciate the greatness of their country unless they understand the true story of its founding, as related with great clarity and conviction by this group of noted Christian historians. Speakers include: Dr. Paul Jehle, Doug Phillips, William Potter, Dr. Joseph Morecraft III, and Jonathan Falwell.

Format: DVD (21)

Resource for: Age 10 to adult

Subjects: U.S. History, Theology

An Encouragement: *This collection from the Jamestown Quadricentennial*

Celebration held in Williamsburg, Virginia in 2007 is a history unit unto itself. Use it to create a study of early American history, or tie it in with the other Vision Forum history materials.

How the Scots Saved Christendom: Tales of Bravehearts and Covenanters

The heather-clad moors of Scotland have given the world much more than a nation of hardy warriors. Indeed, the peoples of Caledonia have left us a legacy of bravery and manhood, resisting political and religious tyranny and often dyeing glen and loch with martyred blood. *How the Scots Saved Christendom* relates these stories, beginning with the early Christian influence of the island of Iona and the struggle for freedom led by Wallace and Bruce. From here we travel through history, meeting John Knox and Mary, Queen of Scots. Blood flows as we discover the horrible persecution of the Covenanters, known simply as The Killing Time. We learn how Sir Walter Scott reawakened the Scottish spirit, and the tremendous influence of Scotland upon America. More than just a history lesson about Scotland, these messages establish a foundation for extensive research into Christianity and the ongoing struggle for religious freedom. Also included is a taste of Celtic music sung by Charlie Zahm.

Format: CD (12)

Resource for: Age 10 to adult

Subjects: World History, Language Arts, Architecture, Music, Theology

Ideas and Topics for Discussion and Composition

> What is the meaning of sovereign Grace?
>
> William Wallace: Symbol of Freedom and Courage
>
> John Knox: Battles to Fight (Ephesians 6:12)
>
> Iona: Evangelist to America

Further Study

> Divine Right of Kings
>
> Five Articles of Perth
>
> David Livingston
>
> Samuel Rutherford
>
> James Ussher
>
> Robert Burns

2nd Reformation 1638

Bach: Reformation Composer

The Battle of Bothwell Bridge

Additional Vision Forum Resources

Hunted and Harried (book), by R.M. Ballantyne

How God Wants Us to Worship Him (book), by Dr. Joseph Morecraft III

The Life and Campaigns of Stonewall Jackson (book), by Robert Lewis Dabney

The Life and Times of Archbishop James Ussher (book), by J. A. Carr

Reformers & Revolutionaries (10 DVDs)

Let Freedom Ring: The Philadelphia Faith & Freedom Tour

This CD album presents a vivid overview of colonial Pennsylvania and New Jersey, placing particular emphasis on the time period of the American War for Independence. Talks range from the Battles of Brandywine and Trenton to the Continental Congress, the Declaration of Independence and striking personalities such as George Washington, Benjamin Franklin, and the Marquis de Lafayette. Intertwined with discussions regarding the Revolutionary War is a theological discourse about the history of Quakers and an architectural address on the significance of various building styles employed in Philadelphia during the eighteenth century. The messages are delivered by Doug Phillips and historian William Potter.

Resource for: Age 10 to adult

Subjects: U.S. History, Language Arts

An Encouragement: *These messages can be used as a resource for a unit study on the War for Independence, as well as a complement to any U.S. History textbook. The insight into the character and influence of the Founding Fathers presents an encouraging look at the men who were used by God to birth our nation.*

Topics for Composition and Discussion

How the Family-Based Christian Culture was Shattered by the War for Independence

The Paintings of Charles Wilson Peale

The Contrast Between Organic Law and Evolving Law

The Crossing of the Delaware and General Washington

Why the Victories at Trenton and Princeton were the Turning Point of the War

Further Study

Henry Knox

Nathanael Greene

Marquis de Lafayette

Isaac Watts

John Paul Jones

Additional Vision Forum Resources

George Washington: America's Joshua (CD), by Doug Phillips

Independence Day (CD), by Doug Phillips

Landmarks and Liberty: The New England Faith & Freedom Tour (1 MP3 or 8 CDs)

True to the Old Flag (book), by G.A. Henty

The League of Grateful Sons (DVD)

The Birkenhead Drill (book), by Doug Phillips

History of the World Mega-Conference Collection

Nearly one thousand people from around the world gathered to attend History of the World Mega-Conference in 2006, learning about 6,000 years of earth history from a distinctively Christian perspective. The sixty-eight lectures presented by a dozen scholars and historians have impacted tens of thousands in the succeeding years, providing not only a wealth of information on a plethora of subjects, but also inspiring many to dig even deeper into specific areas by studying suggested books, researching the characters presented, and learning about the cultures in which they lived.

History of the World Conference DVD Collection

The ten DVDs contained in this collection are a selection from the best of History of the World Mega-Conference. From the biblical story of Genesis and the empires of Babylon and Greece to the message of the Mayas and the foundation of America as we know it today, these lectures make an excellent foundation for any world history course.

Format: DVD (10)

Resource for: Age 12 to adult

Subjects: World History, U.S. History, Theology

History of the World Study Guide

The companion resource to the DVD collection is extremely helpful for your home education providing introductions to each message, and complete outlines of the topics introduced. Questions are also provided to test your children's comprehension skills, allowing them to think through the issues, and not simply pass a test. Group discussions, further reading sources, Scripture memory passages, helpful word definitions, and lecture summaries are also included.

Format: Book

Resource for: 12 to Adult

Subjects: World History, U.S. History, Theology

History of the World: B.C.

Included in this audio album are twenty lectures covering the first four millennia of earth history. Speaker Doug Phillips begins by laying the foundation for all 6,000 years of earth history from a biblical perspective. He is followed by Dr. John Whitcomb, who presents a historic defense of the Genesis flood, as well as thoughts about the first two millennia and their influence on subsequent ages. Continuing in this chronological fashion, Col. John Eidsmoe teaches about the Hebrew nation, Dr. George Grant explores the meaning of Rome, and William Potter shares fascinating information about historical books and libraries, with many other subjects in between.

Format: CD (20)

Resource for: Age 12 to adult

Subjects: World History, U. S. History, Theology, Science

History of the World: A.D.

The journey through history is continued in this album, covering events from Christ's incarnation to modern times. What young person wouldn't want to learn about the battle of Teutoburg Forest as vividly portrayed by Col. John Eidsmoe, or hear the exciting and insightful presentation by Dr. Marshall Foster on the American Republic? Dr. George Grant also gives a fascinating presentation on understanding Islam and how it has impacted our modern world. Each of these talks emphasize God's providential hand in history, revealing that history is not a collection of boring facts, but an exciting adventure learning the stories of God's plan through the ages.

Resources for: Age 12 to adult

Subjects: World History, U. S. History, Theology, Science

An Encouragement: The complete History of the World Collection can be used as a high school world history course or as a year-long unit study, incorporating language arts, fine arts, music, and science. Although the material presented stresses the subject of history, further study on the subjects listed can be researched for each time period covered. An excellent curriculum for independent study, the truths and insights in these messages also provide many opportunities for family interaction and discussion on issues pertinent to our time.

Listed below each lecture from History *of the World* DVD series is a sampling of other related products from History *of the World Mega-Conference Collection* that will provide additional information for further study.

DVD #1: "Six Thousand Years of Earth History in an Hour," by Doug Phillips

History of the World: B.C. (20 CDs):

#2: "The Greatest Themes of the First Two Millennia of Earth History," by Dr. Paul Jehle

#7: "The Greatest Themes of the Third and Fourth Millennia of Earth History," by Dr. Paul Jehle

History of the World: A.D. (20 CDs):

#1: "The Greatest Themes of the Fifth and Sixth Millennia of Earth History," by Dr. Paul Jehle

DVD #2: "The World That Perished," by Dr. John Whitcomb

History of the World: B.C. (20 CDs):

#3: "A Defense of the Universality of the Genesis Flood," by Dr.

John Whitcomb

#4: "The Implications of the Genesis Flood on Earth History," by Dr. John Whitcomb

#8: "The Tower of Babel and the Dispersion of the Nations," by Dr. John Whitcomb

#20: "The Long War Against God," by Dr. John Whitcomb

Mysteries of the Ancient World (12 CDs):

#4: "The Mystery of the Nephilim Presented: Harbingers of Global Judgment," by Doug Phillips

#5, 6: "The Mystery of the Nephilim Solved: Discovering the True Giants of Past Paganism," by Doug Phillips

DVD #3: "What Every Christian Should Know about the Babylonian Empire," by Dr. Paul Jehle

History of the World: B.C. (20 CDs):

#2: "The Great Themes of the First Two Millennia of Earth History," by Dr. Paul Jehle

#7: "The Great Themes of the 3rd & 4th Millennia of Earth History," by Dr. Paul Jehle

History of the World: A.D. (20 CDs):

#16: "Islam and the Modern World," by Dr. George Grant

Providential Battles: Vol. 1 (4 CDs):

#1: "Arbela (331 B.C.): Macedonia vs. Persians," by William Potter

Mysteries of the Ancient World (12 CDs):

#7, 8: "The Mystery of the Ica Stones and the Nazca Lines: Dragon Riders & Owl Men," by Doug Phillips

DVD #4: "Jerusalem and Athens: Antithesis Between Hebrew and Greek Cultures," by Doug Phillips

Providential Battles: Vol. 1 (4 CDs):

#1: "Salamis (480 B.C.): Greeks vs. Persians," by William Potter

History of the World: B.C. (20 CDs):

#14: "The History of the Hebrew Nation, Pt. 1," by Col. John Eidsmoe

#15: "The History of the Hebrew Culture, Pt. 2," by Col. John Eidsmoe

#17: "The Meaning of Rome," by Dr. George Grant

History of the World: A.D. (20 CDs):

#18: "America's Social Engineers and What They Designed," by Geoffrey Botkin

DVD #5: "Vikings: Their Law, Culture, and Conquest," by Col. John Eidsmore

History of the World: A.D. (20 CDs):

#13: "The History of the Law of Nations, Pt. 1," by Dr. Paul Jehle

#14: "The History of the Law of Nations, Pt. 2," by Dr. Paul Jehle

DVD #6: "Crusaders," by Dr. George Grant

Providential Battles: Vol. 1 (4CDs):

#1: "Tours (732 A.D.): Franks vs. Moors," by William Potter

History of the World: A.D. (20 CDs):

#16: "Islam and the Modern World," by Dr. George Grant

DVD #7: "The Message of the Mayas," by Doug Phillips

History of the World: B.C. (20 CDs):

#10: "The Puzzle of Ancient Man," by Doug Phillips

Mysteries of the Ancient World (12 CDs):

#9, 10, 11: "The Mystery of the Incas," by Doug Phillips

DVD #8: "Jamestown's Legacy of Law and Gospel," by Doug Phillips

History of the World: B.C. (20 CDs):

#19: "Special Providences of God in the Advancement of Christendom," by Doug Phillips

History of the World: A.D. (20 CDs):

#10: "The Global Influence of John Calvin," by Dr. Joseph Morecraft III

DVD #9: "The Miracle of America," by Dr. Marshall Foster

Providential Battles: Vol. 1 (4CDs):

#3: "Saratoga (1777): England vs. United States," by William Potter

#3: "Yorktown (1781): England vs. United States," by William Potter

Providential Battles: Vol. 2 (4 CDs):

#2: "New York City (1776): George Washington vs. Lord William Howe," by William Potter

History of the World: A.D. (20 CDs):

#17: "The American Republic," by Dr. Marshall Foster

DVD #10: "How Families Have Changed the World," by Dr. Marshall Foster

History of the World: A.D. (20 CDs):

#9: "What Every Christian Needs to Know about the Reformation," by Dr. Joseph Morecraft III

Additional Vision Forum Resources

The Dragon and the Raven (book), by G.A. Henty

Winning His Spurs (book), by G.A. Henty

By Right of Conquest (book), by G.A. Henty

True to the Old Flag (book), by G.A. Henty

Christianity & Western Civilization (10 DVDs)

Reformers & Revolutionaries (10 DVDs)

How the Scots Saved Christendom (12 CDs)

A Comprehensive Defense of the Providence of God in the Founding of America (21 DVDs)

Providential Battles I: Twenty Battles that Changed the World

Crash! Bang! Sword and dagger, catapult and cannon, knight and infidel—what can spark a boy's imagination more? Military historian William Potter takes listeners on a tumultuous journey through twenty of history's most important battles, exploring the amazing providences of God displayed in their outcomes. Don your armor, steady your sword, and fight alongside Greeks, Romans, Franks, English, Texans, and many others, from the naval battle of Salamis in 480 B.C. to Stalingrad in 1943. The existence of the world as we know it depends on their results!

Format: CD (4)

Resource for: Age 8 to adult

Subjects: World History, U.S. History

Providential Battles II: Epic Conflicts that Changed the World

In this companion album, William Potter explores eight more monumental battles in detail, once again demonstrating the providence of God, and His hand in the affairs of armies. Included are the battles of: Lutzen, during the Thirty Years War; Naseby, between Cromwell and King Charles I; New York City, Gage vs. Washington; Gaines Mill, Lee against McClellan; Sedan, during the Franco-Prussian War; Tsushima, between the Russians and Japanese; Normandy at D-Day; and the Six Day War between Israel and Egypt, Jordan and Syria. Prepare to be astonished!

Format: CD (4)

Resource for: Age 8 to adult

Subjects: World History, U. S. History

Sabers, Spears, & Catapults: A Providential History of Military Technology

Instead of studying particular battles, *Sabers, Spears, & Catapults* follows the development of military technology during the ages. Sword and spear, bow and catapult give way to saber and bayonet, rifle and cannon. A complete understanding of modern weaponry requires a knowledge of its foundations and the world's changing mindset as more and more destruction becomes possible. Historian William Potter reminds us that God is in control, and that no matter how far weapons may advance, He will never be overcome.

Format: CD (4)

Resource for: Age 8 to adult

Subjects: World History, U. S. History

An Encouragement: Do you have a reluctant history student? How about a battle aficionado? Why not use this series of battle messages to set the stage for a unique study of world history? The following list of battles described by Mr. Potter is in chronological order, and, just for fun, the corresponding Henty adventure novels have been included for your student's further learning and enjoyment!

Location	Date	Opponents	Album/Disc †
Salamis	480 B.C.	Greeks vs. Persians	PB1, Disc 1
Arbela	331 B.C.	Macedonians vs. Persians	PB1, Disc 1
Cannae	216 B.C.	Romans vs. Carthaginians	PB1, Disc 1
			*The Young Carthaginian**
"Wars, Warriors, and Weapons of Bible Times"			SSC, Disc 1
Tours	732 A.D.	Muslims vs. Franks	PB1, Disc 1
Crecy	1346 A.D.	England vs. France	PB1, Disc 2
			*St. George for England**
			*At Agincourt**
"Agincourt: Longbows, Swords, and the End of an Era"			SSC, Disc 2
Constantinople	1453 A.D.	Eastern Romans vs. Turks	PB1, Disc 2
Tenochtitlan	1521 A.D.	Spanish vs. Aztecs	PB1, Disc 2
			*By Right of Conquest**
Lepanto	1571 A.D.	Europe vs. Arab Fleet	PB1, Disc 2
Armada	1588 A.D.	England vs. Spain	PB1, Disc 2
			*By England's Aid**
Lutzer	1632 A.D.	The Thirty Years War	PB2, Disc 1
			*The Lion of the North**
			*Won by the Sword**
Naseby	1645 A.D.	English Civil War	PB2, Disc 1
			*Friends Though Divided**

Quebec	1759 A.D.	England vs. France	PB1, Disc 3
			*With Wolfe in Canada**
New York City	1776 A.D.	U.S. War for Independence	PB2, Disc 2
			*True to the Old Flag**
Saratoga	1777 A.D.	U.S. War for Independence	PB1, Disc 3
Yorktown	1781 A.D.	U.S. War for Independence	PB1, Disc 3
Trafalgar	1805 A.D.	England vs. France	PB1, Disc 3
			*At Aboukir and Acre**
			*The Young Buglers**
Waterloo	1815 A.D.	England vs. France	PB1, Disc 3
			*One of the 28th**
"Waterloo: The Gun Powder Revolution's Great Harvest"			SSC
Alamo	1836 A.D.	Texans vs. Mexico	PB1, Disc 4
Antietam	1862 A.D.	War Between the States	PB1, Disc 4
			*With Lee in Virginia**
Gaines Mill	1862 A.D.	War Between the States	PB2, Disc 2
Sedan	1870 A.D.	Franco-Prussian War	PB2, Disc 3
			*The Young Franc-Tireurs**
Tsushima	1905 A.D.	Russo-Japanese War	PB2, Disc 3
1st Marne	1914 A.D.	World War I	PB1, Disc 4
"The Somme: Mechanical Massacre in the 20th Century"			SSC
Britain	1940 A.D.	World War II	PB1, Disc 4
Midway	1942 A.D.	World War II	PB1, Disc 4
Stalingrad	1942-43 A.D.	World War II	PB1, Disc 4
Normandy	1944 A.D.	World War II	PB2, Disc 4
Six Day War	1969 A.D.	Israel vs. Arab Nations	PB2, Disc 4

† Album title abbreviations for *Providential Battles* Vols. 1 & 2, and *Sabers, Spears, & Catapults*

* Titles by G.A. Henty

Additional Vision Forum Resources

Sergeant York and the Great War (book), edited by Tom Skeyhill and "Little Bear" Wheeler

The League of Grateful Sons (DVD)

Bible Lessons for Manhood from the Battlefield of My Father's Youth (6 CDs)

Coming In on a Wing and a Prayer (book), by Kelly Bradrick (née Brown)

Mysteries of the Ancient World

The ancient world is full of mystery and uncertainty. What were the Nephilim? Why did the Nazca people spend so much time creating enormous geometric figures that could only be seen from the sky? Doug Phillips explores these and many more questions in his journey through the ancient world, including the account of origins in Genesis, the attraction of the moon to pagan worshippers, the Ica Stones, Machu Picchu, and much more. Following are the messages included in this series.

1. The Mystery of Origins: The Cosmic Implications of Creation *Ex Nihilo*

2. The Mystery of the Moon: From Godsend to Goddess

3. The Mystery of the Nephilim Presented: Harbingers of Global Judgment

4. The Mystery of the Nephilim Solved: Discovering the True Giants of Paganism Past

5. The Mystery of the Ica Stones and the Nazca Lines: Dragon Riders and Owl Men

6. The Mystery of the Incas: Machu Picchu and the Lost Legacy of the Stone Masons

7. The Mystery of the Galápagos: Laboratory of Evolution or Testimony to Creation?

Format: CD (12)

Resource for: Age 10 to adult (some mature themes)

Subjects: World History, Creation Science, Astronomy, Mathematics, Theology

An Encouragement: These messages are a fantastic example of how to

defend some of the theological, scientific, and historical questions that assault Christians today. Doug Phillips takes his listeners on a journey around the ancient world and shares insights gleaned from his personal study and observations. An excellent stand-alone study resource, this CD series can also be integrated into any world history or creation science study.

Ideas and Topics for Composition and Discussion

Write your own "Book of Beginnings" about your family legacy.

Interview someone who remembers "Man's First Step on the Moon."

Is Ancient Man Superior to Modern Man?

Why Genesis is Needed to Understand the New Testament

The Nephilim and the Bible

Paganism and the Twenty-First Century

The Downfall of the Mayan Civilization

The Legacy of Hiram Bingham

How the Animals Came to the Galápagos Islands

Further Study

First Law of Thermodynamics

Solar System

Table of Nations

Cortez and the Aztecs

Pizzarro and the Incas

Admiral Fitzroy

Additional Vision Forum Resources

The Mysterious Islands (DVD)

Jonathan Park Goes to the Galápagos (4 CDs)

Top Ten Questions about Genesis and Creation (DVD), by Ken Ham

Destination: Moon (book), by James Irwin

Christian Controversies Collection in American History

Many Christians will boldly proclaim their appreciation for the faith of our American spiritual fathers and the hand of God in our history, but when confronted by skeptics and humanists, the same Christians will sheepishly retreat, unable to answer the most basic questions concerning our nation's past. How can we defend our liberty if we are ignorant of its origins and unable to refute the theologically flimsy and historically dishonest arguments of those who minimize our Christian heritage? Enter the Vision Forum Christian Controversies in America History Series—five CDs (60-90 min. each) addressing some of the most hotly debated topics in American history from a biblical and scholarly perspective. These CDs may be purchased individually or as a set.

Pilgrims vs. Indians

A survey of the history of relations between the Pilgrims and the Indians from 1620 to 1670 disproves the modern view that the Pilgrims engaged in genocide. As detailed by Doug Phillips, the Pilgrims' dealings with the Indians were marked by peace, commerce, and a desire to share the gospel of Jesus Christ. This message looks at both Pilgrim and Indian cultures in early colonial times and concludes that the relations between the two communities represented the high water mark of Christian/Indian relations in North America.

Format: CD

Resources for: Age 10 to adult

Subjects: U.S. History, Theology

Puritans vs. Witches

This talk gives an excellent and balanced view of the nine-month period in 1692 when the Puritan leaders of Salem, Massachusetts conducted the infamous "Witch Trials." The points stressed are the biblical wrongness of witchcraft, the sin of bitterness which led to unfounded denunciations, and the deviations from the common law principles based on Scripture of an accused person being presumed innocent until proven guilty. Speaker Dr. Paul Jehle also puts forth the theory that God used these trials to lay the foundation for the greatest revival in American history—the Great Awakening

Format: CD

Resources for: Age 10 to adult

Subjects: U.S. History, Theology

Christians vs. Deists

In *Christians vs. Deists*, Dr. Joseph Morecraft III effectively disproves the modern notion that most of our Founding Fathers were merely deists in Deists in the Enlightenment tradition. He presents convincing evidence of the influence of the Scottish Reformation on those who drafted our founding documents, and depicts the Founders as real men who operated in a distinctively Christian and Calvinistic cultural consensus. His candid assessment of Thomas Jefferson is of special interest.

Format: CD

Resources for: Age 12 to adult

Subjects: U.S. History, Theology

Patriots vs. Tories

This lecture tackles the challenging issue of whether the American Revolutionary War was biblically justified. In addressing this subject, Dr. Morecraft conducts a broad overview of the biblical and historical Reformation perspective, touching on Old Testament Israel and the principle of submission to authority as articulated in Romans 13. He skillfully charts key elements such as the Geneva Bible, the Westminster Confession, and the teachings of John Calvin and the French Huguenots which so greatly influenced the thinking of the American leaders in the 1770s.

Format: CD

Resources for: Age 10 to adult

Subjects: U.S. History, Theology

Yankees vs. Rebels

This fresh, detailed review of the underlying factors that led to the War Between the States will spur many to re-evaluate their understanding of the cause of this conflict. Historian William Potter traces the background and development preceding the war while discussing the issues of slavery, sectional differences, and the conflict between states rights and centralized federal government. This talk is sprinkled with treatments of significant figures of the era, from Nat Turner to Daniel Webster to John Brown, helping to make the subject and the time period come alive. Listen to learn the true series of events that slowly escalated into the first and only civil war in our nation's history.

Format: CD

Resource for: Age 10 to adult

Subjects: U.S. History, Theology

An Encouragement: The Christian Controversies in American History collection should be listened to by all families desiring a proper understanding of these issues, each of which is being wrongly presented today in the context of political correctness. Arm your family with the truth based upon proper historical and biblical analysis. This audio series makes a great complement to any U.S. history course, and is an excellent framework for a unit study or for a family discussion.

Additional Vision Forum Resources

History of the World (10 DVDs)

History of the World: B.C. (20 CDs)

History of the World: A.D. (20 CDs)

Christianity & Western Civilization (10 DVDs)

Reformers & Revolutionaries (10 DVDs)

Poems for Patriarchs (book), edited by Doug Phillips

The Life and Campaigns of Stonewall Jackson (book), by Robert Lewis Dabney

Christ in the Camp (book), by J. William Jones

Line in the Sand: The Texas Faith & Freedom Tour

The story of the Alamo is just the tip of the iceberg when it comes to Texas history. Here is an opportunity to learn of the European antecedents that precipitated Spanish conquest, the rise of Mexican hegemony, the battles in the fight for Texas Independence, and stirring tales of the Texas Rangers and Teddy Roosevelt and the Rough Riders. Outstanding figures from Texas history are candidly yet respectfully examined, including Moses and Stephen Austin, Sam Houston, and Admiral Chester A. Nimitz. The messages are presented in nearly ten hours of audio by speakers, Doug Phillips, William Potter, Wesley Strackbein, and Bill and Scott Brown.

Format: MP3

Resource for: Age 10 to adult

An Encouragement: Not only will this material make you quite knowledgeable about Texas history, it makes a great U.S. History course to show the worldview, determination, courage, and fortitude of the pioneers who settled our nation. Illustrating the independent spirit that has become a Texas legacy, and challenging us to be willing to stake a stand for biblical truth, this series provides a vast array of subjects for study.

Ideas and Topics for Composition and Discussion

The Multigenerational Vision of the Austin Men

A Line in the Sand: Through the Generations

Heroes of the Alamo

The Rough Riders and the Spanish American War

Robert Lewis Dabney and Feminism

Admiral Nimitz: A Texas Hero

The Texas Brigade and the Civil War

Write a letter detailing your personal vision for life.

Interview your parents to chronicle the battles they have fought to preserve your family.

Further Study

Sam Houston

Santa Anna

Andrew Jackson

Texas Rangers

Metaphysical Club

Journal of Mary Maverick

Jim Bowie Knife

Additional Vision Forum Resources

Christianity & Western Civilization (10 DVDs):

#9: "Competing Views of Dominion: Roman Catholic vs. Reformed," by Dan Ford

Providential Battles: Vol. 1 (4 CDs):

#4: "Alamo" (1836), by William Potter

Providential Battles: Vol. 2 (4 CDs):

#2: "Gaines Mill" (1862), by William Potter

With Lee in Virginia (book), by G.A. Henty

The League of Grateful Sons (DVD)

Coming In on a Wing and a Prayer (book), by Kelly Bradrick (née Brown)

Robert Lewis Dabney: The Prophet Speaks (book), edited by Doug Phillips

George Washington: America's Joshua

God creates nations, and God raises up men for critical times in those nations' histories. George Washington was the man God raised up to aid the colonists in their War for Independence from the tyranny of Great Britain. This message explores Washington's role as America's "Joshua" as he led the military operations that eventually wrested our land from England's harsh grasp. Specifically, Doug Phillips focuses on the necessary qualities found in a truly successful leader, the most important of which is the fear of the Lord. In addition, several of the most controversial or interesting aspects of this great man's life are covered, such as his role as a Mason, his interactions with the Continental Congress, and the Conway Cabal.

Format: CD

Subjects: U.S. History, Theology

An Encouragement: *The purpose of this talk is to show how George Washington exemplified many of the character qualities found in Scripture. Use as a complement to a study on George Washington and/or the American colonial time period. Also makes an excellent study on leadership.*

Additional Vision Forum Resources

Robert Lewis Dabney: The Prophet Speaks (book), edited by Doug Phillips

Christians vs. Deists (CD), by Dr. Joseph Morecraft III

Patriots vs. Tories (CD), by Dr. Joseph Morecraft III

6,000 Years of Earth History

This is a whirlwind overview of the history of mankind, emphasizing that God is faithful to fulfill his promises and that He works through families.

As Doug Phillips traces the story of God's unfolding plan through the centuries, he whets your appetite to delve deeper into the study of figures such as John Wycliffe, Martin Luther, and Charles Darwin. An excellent foundational resource for developing an understanding of God's abiding grace through the ages.

Format: CD

Subjects: World History, Theology

Science & Creationism

We desire our children to understand that all truth about our physical universe is tied to creation by a sovereign and almighty God, and that the teaching of science must be consistent with Scripture. The following materials produced by Vision Forum help to prepare our children to defend the faith through the area of science.

Back to Genesis: In the Beginning, God

The Book of Genesis is not only foundational to an understanding of all the books of the Bible, but to having a proper biblical worldview as well. This first book of the Bible was even a fundamental foundation for the laws of England, upon which our America legal system is based, as argued by famous commentator Sir William Blackstone. Therefore, when the doctrines found in the Book of Beginnings are attacked, we must rise and defend them. In *Back to Genesis*, Doug Phillips and Dr. John Morris stand shoulder to shoulder as they present a normative, historical, and grammatical understanding of the Genesis account of origins.

Format: CD (9)

Resource for: Age 10 to adult

Subjects: Science, Theology

Topics for Composition and Discussion

Genesis and the War of the Worldviews

The Dangerous Doctrine of Progressive Creationism

Dinosaurs and the Ark

The Six Days of Creation

Further Study

Bacteria

Virus

Rationalism

Mt. St. Helens

Tsunami

Fossils

Mutations

Additional Vision Forum Resources

Jonathan Park Creation Adventure Audio Library (7 CD albums)

Jonathan Park Guide Set (3 CD albums)

The Mysterious Islands (DVD)

Calvin vs. Darwin: The Battle of the Millennium (DVD)

The Mysterious Islands

When Charles Darwin boarded the *HMS Beagle* and sailed for the Galápagos Islands, the world would never be the same. His book, *On the Origin of the Species*, which described his Theory of Evolution, has detrimentally impacted millions of men, women, and children. In *The Mysterious Islands*, Doug Phillips and a team of filmmakers and Christian scientists travel back to the Galápagos Islands, often called the "Laboratory of Evolution," determined to prove Darwin wrong. Discover ancient tortoises, salt-sneezing marine iguanas, flightless cormorants, and many more species, each without fear of man. Watch this visually stunning journey through the beautiful Galápagos Islands as you learn about the fallacies of the evolutionism arguments put forth by Darwin and his followers.

Format: DVD

Resource for: Family

Subjects: Science, Sociology, History

An Encouragement: Definitely a DVD to watch together as a family. The scene featuring Admiral Fitzroy's bold defense of Scripture is my favorite! The quallity of photography is exceeded only by the film's message as Doug Phillips and his son, Joshua, share their adventures on the Galápagos Islands.

Further Study

Margaret Sanger

Planned Parenthood

Natural Selection

Animals of the Galápagos Islands

Additional Vision Forum Resources

Jonathan Park Goes to the Galápagos (4 CDs)

Jonathan Park Vol. 4: The Hunt for Beowulf (4 CDs)

Calvin vs. Darwin: The Battle of the Millennium (DVD)

The Top Ten Questions about Genesis and Creation

To completely accept the truths of the Bible, we must believe that it is the infallible Word of God. When worldly "Christians" try to reinterpret Genesis to fit modern evolutionism ideas, they are actually fighting a battle against God. If your children can't defend their beliefs, they too will begin to doubt. Australian Ken Ham has spent his life providing answers to questions from Christians and unbelievers alike, and has founded a ministry called Answers in Genesis, which recently built a technologically-advanced Creation Museum in Kentucky. In *The Top Ten Questions about Genesis and Creation*, Ken Ham answers some of the most common queries that Christians will be asked. These include:

The age of earth—does it matter?

Is there evidence for an Infinite God?

Where did Cain find his wife?

How could Noah fit all the species of animals on the ark?

How did the different "races" of people come about?

Format: DVD

Resource for: Family

Subjects: Science, Theology, History

An Encouragement: *Watch this DVD, and then have your students answer its question, either in written form or through discussion, so as to implant these truths in the minds of your entire family.*

Additional Vision Forum Resources

Jonathan Park Vol. 1: The Adventure Begins:

#1: "Adventure on the Aucilla River"

Jonathan Park Vol. 2: No Looking Back:

#1: "The Bone of Contention"

Jonathan Park Vol. 3: The Winds of Change:

#2: "The Temple of the Moon"

Darwin vs. Calvin: The Battle of the Millennium

Ladies and gentlemen! Presenting the battle of the worldviews! The principles of Charles Darwin, particularly the Theory of Evolution, have had world-shaking consequences in the 150 years since the publication of his book, *On the Origin of Species.* On the other hand we have John Calvin, firm defender of biblical truths and expounder of God's Word, who greatly aided in destroying the heresy of Roman Catholicism during the Protestant Reformation. During this historic debate, both men are given the opportunity to defend their respective worldviews and disprove their opponent's. Be prepared for a fun, informative, and often spirited exchange.

Format: DVD

Resource for: Family

Subjects: Science, History, Language Arts, Theology

An Encouragement: *This DVD can be used as a complement to any study on creationism vs. evolutionism, and also on the Reformation.*

Additional Vision Forum Resources

Back to Genesis (9 CDs)

The Bioeithics of Life Collection (5 DVDs)

Reformers & Revolutionaries (10 DVDs)

Christianity & Western Civilization (10 DVDs)

Jonathan Park Creation Adventure Audio Library (7 CD Albums)

Every year, thousands of boys and girls all around the world ask the same question: "When will the next Jonathan Park come out?" Children sit breathlessly on the edge of their seats as Jonathan and his family travel the world in search of exciting testimonies of God's creation, which invariably involves them in adventures of epic proportions. Meet the members of the Creation Response Team, and learn what drives these dedicated Christians to defend the Bible as they encounter hostile Darwinists, volcanoes, plane crashes, and even a few modern-day pirates!

Jonathan Park Volume I: The Adventure Begins

When Jonathan Park and his father meet the Brenan family in a hidden cave, they find much more than just shelter from the storm outside. After discovering a massive dinosaur graveyard, these two families combine forces to build a Creation Science Museum to spread the message of the Creator!

Ideas and Topics for Composition and Discussion

Research rapid geological changes caused by Noah's Flood.

Discuss advanced intelligence from early civilizations.

Write about the dispersion of people groups at the Tower of Babel.

What happened to all the dinosaurs?

Can aliens exist and the Bible still be true?

Further Study

Fossilization and Dinosaur Graveyards

Four Creation Scientists: Robert Boyle, Isaac Newton, Samuel Morse, and Wernher von Braun

Supposed "Ape-Man" Fossils: Neanderthals, Cro-Magnon,

Macro-evolution vs. Micro-evolution

Fibonacci Numbers

Charles Darwin

Additional Vision Forum Resources

Christianity and Science Fiction (DVD), by Doug Phillips

History of the World: B.C. (20 CDs):

#8: "The Tower of Babel and the Dispersion of the Nations," by Dr. John Whitcomb

Jonathan Park Volume II: No Looking Back

Join the Parks and Brenans as they continue to build a museum that presents the true story of Creation. From the tottering heights of a railroad bridge to arsons and kidnappers, I promise you it will be a wild ride!

Topics for Composition and Discussion

How old is the earth, and why is that important?

Why are there so many fossilized clams?

What is a scientific theory?

How do the amazing designs we see in animals support a Creator?

Further Study

Mt. St. Helens

Animals: Woodpeckers, Horses, Bats, Wolves, Owls, Lions, Giraffes, Ostriches, Toucans, Hippopotamuses, Elephants, Spiders

The Water Cycle

First and Second Laws of Thermodynamics

Sound Waves

Petrification

Jonathan Park Volume III: The Winds of Change

Dr. Kendall Park and his wife, Angela, have made a huge decision: they're going to homeschool their children! Not only this, but the Parker and Brenan families are starting the Creation Response Team, trained by the disaster-response professional Myles Morgan. Hurricanes, bears, and angry Iraqis—the challenges are many. Can the Parks and Brenans make it through alive?

Ideas and Topics for Composition and Discussion

Talk about the difference between the New Age idea of Creator (Earth), and the Christian idea of Creator (God).

What is the difference between a hurricane and a tornado?

Why do we have different languages if we came from the same two people?

Read about the Apollo Space Missions.

What does the Bible mean when it speaks of "kinds" of animals?

Further Study

Fulgurites

New Age Religions

Evolutionist Theories: Punctuated Equilibrium, Chaos Theory

The Ice Age

The Grand Canyon

The Solar System

Animals: Salmon, Polar Bears, Caribou, Porcupines

Additional Vision Forum Resources

Destination: Moon (b00), by Astronaut James Irwin

Mysteries of the Ancient World (12 CDs):

#2, 3: "The Mystery of the Moon," by Doug Phillips

The Top Ten Questions about Genesis and Creation (DVD), by Ken Ham

History of the World: B.C. (20 CDs):

#6: "The History of the Ice Age," by Dr. John Morris

#9: "One Blood: The Origin of the Races," by Dr. John Morris

Jonathan Park Volume IV: The Hunt for Beowulf

The original copy of the famous manuscript *Beowulf* has been stolen from the British Library, and it's up to the Creation Response Team to find the thief. Join the adventure as they track a mysterious Japanese-American to the black sands of Iwo Jima, the sweltering jungles of the Yucatan, the famous Galápagos Islands, and beyond! But watch out. Someone else wants this artifact too, and he won't stop at anything!

Topics for Composition and Discussion

Is it possible that the hundreds of ancient dragon legends from around the world have their basis in a time when man and dinosaur lived together?

What does the word "dinosaur" mean?

What are the similarities between the Mayan account of the world's beginning and that of the Bible?

What are biomes?

Further Study

Beowulf

Iwo Jima

Volcanoes

Navajo Code-Talkers

Animals: Humpback Whales, Sand Tiger Sharks, Jellyfish, Armadillos, Spider Monkeys, Yucca Moth, Finches, Flightless Cormorant, Iguanas, Monarch Butterflies, Hummingbirds, Roadrunners, Skunks,

Symbiotic Relationships

Mutations

The Scopes Trial

Additional Vision Forum Resources

The League of Grateful Sons (DVD)

History of the World DVD Collection:

#7: "The Message of the Mayas," by Doug Phillips

The Mysterious Islands (DVD)

Jonathan Park Volume V: The Explorer's Society

The Creation Response Team has been challenged to a "Battle of the Worldviews" by an evolutionary organization called "The Explorer's Society." Each team has an opportunity to present its worldview before a television audience of millions. Both are ready, and determined to win. The competition is fierce as they travel from freezing Arctic wastelands to boiling black smokers, dogged by the CRT's arch-nemesis. Can the CRT get past sabotage, technical difficulties, and harsh natural conditions to win the prize and spread the creation message?

Topics for Composition and Discussion

Charles Lyell said that "the present is the key to understanding the past." What is wrong with this statement?

How do the many layers of rock laid down by the eruption of Mount St. Helens offer proof for a young earth?

Why have evolutionists not been able to create life?

Further Study

Important Scientists who Believed in the Bible: Robert Boyle, John Ray, Johannes Kepler, Matthew Maury

Uniformitarianism

Niagara Falls

Carbon Dating

Cambrian Explosion

Mt St. Helens

Tetrapods

Biogenesis

Jonathan Park Volume VI: The Journey Never Taken

A rare medallion, a secret message, and two villainous-looking men. What do these have in common? Find out as the Parks and Brenans embark on a mysterious, globe-encompassing treasure hunt. Their path leads them through the legacies of Evolutionism's founding fathers as they desperately research each clue to find the next one's hiding place. But they are not alone in their quest.

Topics for Composition and Discussion

Is there evidence against the Big Bang?

Why do some people believe the myth that Darwin accepted God on his deathbed?

Further Study

Binomial Nomenclature

Erasmus Darwin

George Cuvier

James Hutton

George Young

HMS Beagle

The Galápagos Islands

> Robert Fitzroy
>
> Gregor Mendel
>
> Karl Marx
>
> Ernest Haeckel
>
> John Dewey
>
> Francis Galton

Additional Vision Forum Resources

> *Darwin vs. Calvin* (DVD)
>
> *The Mysterious Islands* (DVD)
>
> *Jonathan Park Goes to the Galápagos* (4 CDs)

Visit JonathanPark.com for more information, fun activities, sample episodes, and free album study guides.

Jonathan Park Volume VII: The Voyage Beyond

In *The Voyage Beyond*, Jonathan and the Creation Response Team meet an eccentric philanthropist-explorer named Alexander DeMarcus. Mr. DeMarcus appears to have a passion for marine life, exploring the ocean depths with his experimental electromagnetic submarine, The Manta. At first the CRT joins forces with Mr. DeMarcus, excited to learn more about God's amazing creatures beneath the sea. But the team soon realizes that this mysterious explorer has something even bigger in mind. Discover his incredible secret in *Jonathan Park and the Voyage Beyond*.

Resource for: Age 6 to adult

Subjects: Science, History

An Encouragement: This is one of my all-time favorite homeschooling resources! I was amazed at the science my son learned just by listening to these audio dramas. Why not encourage your children to write their own episodes as a special school project?

Jonathan Park Guide Set (3 CD Albums)

These albums are not part of the continuing Jonathan Park storyline, but feature some of the same primary characters as the adventure series. They are fun, stand-alone albums that have been produced to help highlight amazing attributes given to God's creatures by their Creator, and to dispel the evolutionary myths created by man.

Format: CD (4)

Resource for: Age 6 to adult

Subjects: Science

Jonathan Park Goes to the Aquarium

This album features 100 mini episodes (approximately 2 minutes each) about some of the most popular marine creatures. Jonathan Park and his father walk through the aquarium, talking about the animals they see, and how they support a biblical account of Creation. Filled with fantastic sound effects and amazing scientific tidbits, this is great to listen to before, after, or during a trip to your local aquarium.

Jonathan Park Goes to the Zoo

Similar in style to *Jonathan Park Goes to the Aquarium*, this album features another 100 mini-episodes (approximately 2 minutes each), this time starring 100 land animals found in most zoos. Did you know that an eagle can spot a running rabbit from a mile away? That's incredible, but so is the polar bear, who can smell a seal three feet under the ice from ten football fields away! Learn more about these and the other amazing creatures presented in *Jonathan Park Goes to the Zoo*.

Jonathan Park Goes to the Galápagos

The Galápagos Islands have long been called the "laboratory for evolution." This mysterious archipelago has been a stopping place for whalers, pirates, and possibly even Incas, but it is also home to a number of incredible animal species. In this album, Dr. Kendall Park and Jonathan travel to "Las Encantadas," or "the Enchanted Islands," as they have been called, to research its flora and fauna, and discover evidence that proves Darwin was wrong. Meet lovable sea lions, gigantic Galápagos tortoises, and exotic blue-footed boobies, debate Darwinist tour-guides, and enjoy the colorful islands' history in this fun and informative autdio guide!

An Encouragement: Going to the aquarium or zoo? Listen to one of the Jonathan Park guides first to familiarize your children with the creatures they'll see, and to instill the true story of those creatures' origins, before reading the normally evolutionistic perspective presented by aquariums and zoos. If you are studying creationism and evolutionism, Jonathan Park Goes to the Galápagos *is a wonderful education resource that will likely hold your child's attention far longer than a normal textbook would.*

Destination: Moon

Astronaut James Irwin was the eighth man to walk on the moon. His voyage was more than physical, however, as he viewed the wonders of the solar system and realized just how much they proclaim the glory of their Creator. Irwin's account of his remarkable adventure is fascinating and informative, giving a brief outline of the history of space exploration, and a more detailed account of his personal experience, as well as the opportunities it gave him later to share the gospel all over the world.

Format: Book

Resource for: Age 6 to adult

Subjects: Science, Astronomy

Topics for Composition and Discussion

> The Solar System
>
> The Moon
>
> John Glenn and Project Mercury
>
> Requirements for Astronauts
>
> Weightlessness

Further Study

> Sputnik
>
> John Glenn
>
> YF-12A
>
> Astronomy
>
> Geology
>
> Centrifuge
>
> Apollo 1
>
> Volcano

Additional Vision Forum Products

> *Jonathan Park: The Winds of Change* (4 CDs):
>> #3: "Destination Moon, Pts. 1 & 2"

PART 4
CHRISTIANITY AND CULTURE

For the weapons of our warfare are not carnal, but mighty through God to the pulling down of strong holds; Casting down imaginations, and every high thing that exalteth itself against the knowledge of God, and bringing into captivity every thought to the obedience of Christ . . . —II Cor. 10:4-5

For the homeschooling family, the Three C's: Christianity, Culture and Curriculum are necessarily intertwined. In our own family, we wanted our children's curriculum to encourage a personal relationship with Jesus Christ and to include instruction on the principles set forth in Scripture, thereby equipping them to engage the culture for the Glory of God. So, we needed to provide a curriculum that presented an understanding of who God is and how He desires us to live. The resources in this section will help your family be better prepared to understand God and His ways as you impact the culture around you through:

Family Life and Discipleship   **The Art of Film**

Theology and Evangelism   **Business and Commerce**

Government and Law

Family Life & Discipleship

Christians are called to be fruitful and multiply and to govern the world around them. In that context we are also to make disciples. In light of these commands from Scripture, we have a responsibility to teach a biblical understanding of the culture of family life and discipleship in our home education. The following products will challenge you personally in your own walk with the Lord, and provide instruction on how to prepare the next generation to establish godly homes.

Safely Home

Offering concrete biblical solutions to the crises in our culture in the areas of family, church and education, author Tom Eldredge makes an insightful comparison between the Greek (humanistic) and the Hebrew (Christian) styles of family life and education. As he highlights these philosophies through history, he encourages us not to live under the bondage of misplaced priorities, wrong lifestyle choices, family segregation and youth-driven church cultures.

Format: Book

Resource for: Parents and young adults

Subjects: History, Home Economics

An Encouragement: Having read many resources on the family, church, and home education, my husband and I still find this to be one of the best. We constantly need to be reminded that the culture in which we live has been tremendously impacted by Greco-Roman philosophies. Reading Mr. Eldredge's description of the Greek culture, which so easily gave up family autonomy to the government because of a desire to live more comfortably and to increase wealth, we see an age that disturbingly mirrors our own time.

Read this to be sure you understand how modern education has been impacted by wrong philosophies. Included below are reviews of other products with a similar theme.

Additional Vision Forum Resources

The Blessed Marriage (CD), by Doug Phillips

The Ministry of Marriage (CD), by Dr. Voddie Baucham

How to Disciple Your Family: A Plan for Generational Victory (10 DVDs)

Building a Family That Will Stand (7 CDs)

The Centrality of the Home (CD), by Dr. Voddie Baucham

Hospitality: The Biblical Commands (CD), by Alexander Strauch

The Family Table (CD), by Doug Phillips

Give Me Your Heart My Son (8 CDs)

The Little Boy Down the Road (book), by Doug Phillips

The Letters and Lessons of Theodore Roosevelt for His Sons (book), compiled and edited by Doug Phillips

Bible Letters of John Quincy Adams for His Son (book), compiled and edited by Douglas Phillips

The Four P's (CD), by Dr. Voddie Baucham

Making Wise Decisions About College (CD), by Doug Phillips

The Blessed Marriage

Marriage is normative and a blessing from God. So asserts Doug Phillips as he makes his case from Scripture, reinforced by anecdotes from his life and the lives of men such as Charles Spurgeon. This message is a refreshing challenge and reminder to think about marriage as God views it, and to cultivate a spirit of appreciation and gratitude for this gift from

God.

Format: CD

Resource for: Age 8 to adult

Subjects: Home Economics, Theology

An Encouragement: A beautiful message to listen to with your spouse, or by yourself, as an encouragement to joyfully live out God's design for marriage. This CD can also be used as a teaching tool to provide your children a biblical vision of marriage as an example of Christ and His relationship to the Church. Why not do a family Bible study using Scripture references relating to marriage?

The Ministry of Marriage

Do not put off marriage for ministry—marriage is ministry! So teaches Dr. Voddie Baucham as he seeks to correct, through a careful review of Scripture, the mistaken notion that staying single is somehow more spiritual than being married. This talk also offers words of exhortation and encouragement to single young ladies who have despaired of ever having a godly husband.

Format: CD

Resource for: Age 8 to adult

How to Disciple Your Family: A Plan for Generational Victory

Encouraging families to plan and implement strategic discipleship goals that will encourage children and grandchildren to live lives of obedience and victory before the Lord, speakers Doug Phillips and Geoffrey Botkin provide a multitude of practical examples gleaned from their own family discipleship experiences. Topics discussed include how to equip your children to think like creative entrepreneurs, how to pass on your convictions generationally, and how to make brothers and sisters best friends.

Format: DVD (10)

Resource for: Fathers

Building a Family That Will Stand

Join Doug Phillips, Phil Lancaster, and John Thompson as they instruct men on how to exercise biblical leadership in their homes. Some of the topics include:

> The Meaning of Patriarchy
>
> Busy Fathers As Family Shepherds
>
> Preparing Sons for Marriage
>
> Biblical Discipline
>
> Family Worship

Format: CD (7)

Resource for: Age 14 to adult

The Centrality of the Home in Evangelism and Discipleship

In an engaging style that quickly captures the listener's attention, Dr. Voddie Baucham provides a theological understanding of why the home is central to evangelism and discipleship based upon the book of Ephesians. This message is directed both toward children who need Christ and to be discipled in the faith, as well as toward parents who must grasp their biblical responsibility to disciple and evangelize in the home. Dr. Baucham's Scripture-centered message is buttressed by statistics that show the Curch is currently losing between 75% and 88% of professing Christian young people by the end of their first year of college.

Format: CD

Resource for: Age 12 to adult

Hospitality: The Biblical Commands

In this message, Alexander Strauch drives home the point that believers are commanded to practice hospitality. He explains how biblical hospitality is a tangible expression of love with overflowing benefits for everyone involved. He addresses the particular obstacles to hospitality which we face in modern America and offers helpful suggestions on how to develop the habit of hospitality within our homes. As a seasoned elder in the body of Christ, he encourages the training of our children toward a mindset of Christian hospitality.

Format: CD

Resource for: Age 10 to adult

Subjects: Home Economics

The Family Table

The meal table has traditionally been recognized as a place for the family to gather around and rest, discuss issues, and learn. But today's society has relegated this important part of family life to the dustbins of history as something only to be unpacked for Thanksgiving and Christmas. In this lecture, Doug Phillips argues that the dinner table is a place of enormous opportunity for the discipleship of our children, and a place that Christ used throughout His ministry to train his own disciples.

Format: CD

Resource for: Age 10 to adult

Subjects: Home Economics

Give Me Your Heart, My Son

This album offers a wealth of encouragement and instruction for fathers and sons desiring to build a biblical vision for unity and love between the men of a family. It's messages are a compilation of highlights culled from several years of the Vision Forum Ministries Father and Son Retreats. The speakers are men of proven character and leadership, including evangelist and historical re-enactor Richard "Little Bear" Wheeler, Norm Wakefield of Elijah Ministries, Bob Welch of Bible Teaching Ministries, and Doug Phillips of Vision Forum Ministries.

Format: CD set

Resource for: Age 8 to adult

The Little Boy Down the Road

Written by Doug Phillips, this book is a collection of thoughts, anecdotes, and essays on essential components of authentic family life, fleshing out in vignettes and personal reflections the biblical doctrine of the family. Of particular interest are chapters dealing with the role of pets within the family, and a real-life account of one father's efforts to portray the true significance of the Pilgrims in the face of intense "politically correct" opposition.

Format: Book

Resource for: Age 8 to adult

The Letters and Lessons of Theodore Roosevelt for His Sons

This book is a wonderful, first-person introduction to Theodore Roosevelt, perhaps the most family-oriented, energetic figure ever to serve as President of the United States. It is divided into three parts: the first, a selection of letters to his sons, organized by son and chronological order; the second, portions of his autobiographical accounts of childhood episodes, youth, and young manhood, including his time as a rancher out West; and third, various essays and speeches written by Roosevelt which touch on the meaning of character and manhood.

Format: Book

Resource for: Age 10 to adult

The Bible Lessons of John Quincy Adams for His Son

The most notable aspect of this book is the amount of time and effort President Adams expended in extolling the virtues of the Word of God to one of his sons. As mentioned by Doug Phillips in the introduction, the reader will observe some theological deficiencies in these letters, in particular uncertainty expressed by Adams ast to whether the Genesis account is to be understood literally or allegorically. Nonetheless, one cannot help but be impressed with the example of a father seeking to fulfill his duty to train and disciple his son.

Format: Book

Resource for: Age 14 to adult

Subjects: U.S. History, Theology

An Enouragement: This 90-page book is an incredible resource for further study! Use it as an impetus to write letters to your own children expounding on the blessings of the Scriptures! Aspiring poets will particularly enjoy the poem by Adams in the back of the book. If you assign this book for independent study, I would recommend that your student would be well-grounded in biblical creationism before reading.

Topics for Composition and Discussion

The Life of John Quincy Adams

The Bible As History: Universal to Individual

Piety to God: Foundation for All Virtue

Further Study

Institutes of Justinian

Commentaries of Blackstone

Assyrian Empire

Babylonian Empire

Egyptian Empire

Additional Vision Forum Resources

History of the World (10 DVDs)

History of the World: B.C. (20 CDs)

History of the World: A.D. (20 CDs)

Poems for Patriarchs (book), compiled and edited by Doug Phillips

The Letters and Lessons of Theodore Roosevelt for His Sons (book), compiled and edited by Doug Phillips

Ten P's in a Pod

This is a wonderful tale of the travels and adventures of a large family involved in ministry, evangelism, and home education long before home education became a movement. Lovingly written by one of the Pent family children, it recounts with candor and humor the challenges of ten family members in the middle decades of the twentieth century. Crisscrossing the country by faith to minister in word and song, they memorized huge chunks of Scripture as they sought to redeem the time. Through this modern-day classic, Arnold Pent, III, illustrates what can be accomplished when a father has a godly vision and faithfully seeks to implement it.

Format: Book

Resource for: Age 8 to adult

The Four P's

Speaker Dr. Voddie Baucham puts forth this controversial proposition: the young man who wants to marry your daughter should meet the qualifications set forth in Scripture to be an elder. He develops his premise by examining from a biblical perspective the suitor's need to be a prophet, priest, provider and protector.

Format: CD

Resource for: Age 10 to adult

Making Wise Decisions about College

The number of homeschooled young people attending college has risen steadily over the years. Speaker Doug Phillips contends that few of them have carefully considered what the valid reasons for going to college are. This CD examines the pressing questions that students and parents should be asking: "What is true biblical education? What are my reasons for going to college? Do I really need a degree for my vocational pursuits? What is the best way of obtaining a degree?" This lecture graciously challenges students seriously consider the issues involved in receiving a university degree without compromising biblical convictions.

Format: CD

Resource for: Age 14 to adult

Theology & Evangelism

As parents engaged in the process of preparing our children to live out the call of God upon their lives, we want to be sure that the materials we use are based upon the sovereignty of God, provide a proper biblical doctrine of man, and employ educational standards derived from Scripture.

With a deep desire for our family to be faithful to "go out and make disciples of all the nations" by proclaiming the "good news" of the gospel, we are grateful to have the following Vision Forum resources as tools to help us accomplish this goal.

How to Think Like a Christian

Just because someone is a Christian does not mean that he thinks like a Christian. This is the admonition given by Doug Phillips as he surveys the pervasive impact of evolutionary concepts on the modern mind. Listen carefully as Mr. Phillips prepares us to fight this battle of the worldviews.

Format: CD

Resource for: Age 10 to adult

Subjects: Theology, Law, History

An Encouragement: Sometimes it is helpful to write down a list of questions to answer before listening to or watching a resource. Provide copies of these questions to your family to be answered in written form or used for subsequent discussion.

Example:

1. *Be able to define the following words: syncretism, normativity, absolute*

2. *How does the modern Sunday school movement demonstrate evolutionary thought?*

3. *What are the foundations of a Christian worldview?*

Further Study

Clarence Darrow and the Leopold and Leob Case

Homo Sapiens

Cornelius Van Til

G. Stanley Hall

Gnosticism

Additional Vision Forum Resources

The Best of the Witherspoon School of Law and Public Policy (16 CDs)

What's a Girl to Do (CD), by Doug Phillips

Making Wise Decisions about College (CD), by Doug Phillips

The History of the Sunday School Movement (CD), by Doug Phillips

History of the World: B.C. (20 CDs)

The Person of Christ

Dr. Voddie Baucham gives a powerful exposition of the gospel, making the point that salvation only comes through the Christ of the Scriptures. He provides solid answers to common objections that are raised concerning Christ's deity, death, and resurrection. Dr. Baucham's passion for Christ and for the gospel message cannot help but touch the hearts and minds of those who are willing to pay the cost and live out their faith in obedience to God's Word.

Format: DVD

Resource for: Family

Subjects: Theology

An Encouragement: *A true resource for all families desiring to be motivated, willing, and prepared to share the gospel through word and deed. This DVD provides a clear and concise explanation of how to use the Scriptures to bring the gospel to those around us. Dr. Baucham's ability to make the truths of the Bible clear is profound, and yet set forth in a manner that is simple and straight-forward. A critical teaching tool for every Christian family.*

The Culture Wars

Dr Voddie Baucham speaks from the heart, calling all Christians to take a stand in the culture wars as academia and the media seek to impose "tolerance," religious relativism, and philosophical pluralism on those proclaiming the name of Christ. Encouraging Christians to speak the truth with boldness and to effectively share their faith, Dr. Baucham reminds us that all answers to the challenges from our culture are found in Scripture.

Format: DVD

Resource for: Family

Subjects: Theology

Ideas and Topics for Composition and Discussion

Apply 2 Timothy 3:12 to the persecution of Christians in our "tolerant culture" of today.

Christians and the Desire for "Pagan" Respect.

The Law of Non-Contradiction

"God Does Not Need to Borrow Any Man's Fame or Name"

Further Study

Relativism

Intolerance

Pluralism

Absolutes

Additional Vision Forum Resources

The Centrality of the Home in Evangelism and Discipleship (CD), by Dr. Voddie Baucham

Guerilla Apologetics for the Glory of God

Ray Comfort is witty and fun, but more importantly he has a heart for the Lord and a passion for witnessing to the lost. In this message he presents the premise that America is currently under judgment, defending this position faithfully from the Bible. He also discusses the fears commonly experienced when witnessing, and the way in which he counteracts them. Interesting, humorous at times, and extremely thought-provoking.

Format: DVD

Resource for: Family

Subject: Theology

We Cannot But Speak: How to Gain a Passion for Evangelism

Exhorting Christians to have a passion for evangelism is Ray Comfort's "signature" message. His humorous but convicting message highlights several practical, biblical principles on how Christians can become passionate about sharing the gospel with those who are lost.

Format: DVD

Resource for: Family

Subject: Theology

An Encouragement: Guerilla Apologetics *and* We Cannot Speak *not only provide impetus for being faithful in the sharing of the gospel, but also instruct how to do so through specific Scripture verses and personal examples. Together, this set provides a thorough, biblical presentation of the gospel that Christians of all ages can apply.*

Theological Bootcamp I and II

These two CD albums, available separately or as a set, provide more than twelve hours of feasting at the theological table. Foundational issues addressed include the canonicity of Scripture, Bible translations, the doctrines of grace, and the role of God's Law in our world. These materials are helpful to young believers wanting to establish positions on foundational issues, as well as to seasoned Christians looking to strengthen their understanding of essential biblical doctrines. The speakers featured are Doug Phillips, Jeff Pollard, Dr. Kenneth Gentry, and Dr. Michael Butler.

Format: CD

Resource for: Age 12 to adult

Subject: Theology

An Encouragement: If you want your children to be rooted in the foundational doctrines of the faith, be prepared to defend the truths of the Scriptures before cynics, and know how to share the gospel, this set is an excellent tool.

The Devolution of Law

The Law of God applies to every area of life. Most modern Christians have rejected this foundational principle, looking instead to the world's idea of morality. In particular, evolutionary ideas are influencing the degeneration of family life and culture and affecting all areas of life, including theology, art, business, and law. In *The Devolution of Law*, Doug Phillips examines the problem and offers this solution: a fundamental understanding of the Bible, and the application of God's Word to every area of our life.

Format: DVD

Resource for: Age 12 to adult

Subjects: Government, Law, Theology

An Encouragement: In addition to using this DVD as a source for a basic unit study on theology or the foundations of law, this message can be used to present the beauty and order of God's Law and how this Law is a reflection of the Lord Jesus Christ. Also recommended is the personal testimony given by Mr. Phillips as an example of why it is necessary to have a real working biblical knowledge of the Scriptures. What a resource to use with our children!

The Spotless Bride: The Beauty of a Holy Church Dwelling in a Pagan Culture

Here is an exploration of the doctrine of the Church using the biblical imagery of the bride of Christ. Speaker Doug Phillips examines the greatest challenges to the purity of the Church: syncretism and an adulterous outlook. This message helps deepen the appreciation for the need of purity within the Church, and asks the listener whether he is part of the problem or part of the solution.

Format: CD

Resource for: Age 12 to adult

The Role of Children in the Meeting of the Church

According to Doug Phillips, the role of children in the Church is to gather with the rest of the local body of believers during the time of worship. He convincingly points out, from both the Old and New Testaments, that children are to be with their parents, not in Sunday school, "children's church," or "youth group." Further examination reveals that this was the consistent pattern throughout Church history until the last two hundred years. Contrary to modern theories of evolution and psychology, children derive great benefit from worshipping with their family. As always, it is essential that we follow biblical patterns and not methods designed by men.

Format: CD

Resource for: Age 10 to adult

Subjects: Theology

Gossip: The Plague of the Church

In this timeless message, Scott Brown bluntly warns about the dangers of gossip within the Church. Launching on a whirlwind tour of what the Bible has to say about the nature of gossip and the damage it causes, Mr. Brown's sober message includes not only a definition of gossip, but also how often it is disguised. Hope for the believer is offered by explaining the scriptural remedy and spiritual blessings for those who turn away from this plague.

Format: CD

Resource for: Age 12 to adult

Uniting Church & Family

As many of us have turned our hearts toward home and have seen the blessing of families living, working and learning together, we have also come to understand the biblical model of worshipping together. Dr. R.C. Sproul Jr., Doug Phillips, Phil Lancaster, and John Thompson examine this issue as they highlight what the Bible has to say about:

- Youth Groups
- Finding or Starting a Local Assembly

- The Church Local vs. the Church Universal
- Family Ministry
- Men in Leadership
- Patriarchy and the Church
- Church Discipline
- House Assemblies
- Church Government
- Shepherding

Format: CD (10)

Resource for: Age 12 to adult

Additional Vision Forum Resources

Church and Family Unity Series (9 CDs)

The History of the Sunday School Movement

This review of the evolution of the Sunday school movement is a true *tour de force*. Comparing the Hebraic with the Hellenistic educational models, Doug Phillips effectively establishes that the foundations of the Sunday school movement lie in Athens, not Jerusalem. His most compelling observation is that there is no model for Sunday school in the Bible, nor in the first eighteen hundred years of Church history. Rather the age-segregated, youth-perpetuating models of Sunday school have their philosophical origins in evolutionary social theory.

Format: CD

Resource for: Age 10 to adult

Subjects: History, Theology

Additional Vision Forum Products

Safely Home (book), by Tom Eldredge

How Modern Churches are Harming Families (CD), by John Thompson

Uniting Church & Family (10 CDs)

Government & Law

Of all people, Christians in particular should concern themselves with the study of government and law. After all, it is God who places leaders in power and who has given us the Law. The resources described in this section will equip and motivate students to consider these subjects from a biblical vantage point.

The following resources were filmed and recorded at the Witherspoon School of Law and Public Policy. This week-long school is designed to give Christian men a vision for leadership in the home, church, and the gates of the land. The hope is that students, law students, fathers, lawyers, and pastors will receive a strong foundation in the Christian origins of our legal system and be equipped to communicate the continuing relevance of God's Word to law and public policy.

Introduction to Christianity, Law, and Culture

This video curriculum includes messages from Doug Phillips, Chief Justice Roy Moore, Justice Tom Parker, Dr. Paul Jehle, Col. John Eidsmoe, and William Einwechter. Some of the topics include:

Christianity and the Common Law

Covenantal Approach to Jurisdictions

Christianity and the Constitution

The Law of the Nations and American History

Format: CD (12)

Resource for: High School to adult

Subjects: History, American Government, Theology, Law

Witherspoon School of Law and Public Policy (2008)

This audio curriculum includes messages from Doug Phillips, Howard Phillips, Chief Justice Roy Moore, William Einwechter, Don Hart, Esq., Bob Renaud, and more. Some of the topics included are:

The Bible and Female Magistrates

Christianity and the Courts

The Battle for Biblical Marriage

Genesis and Geneva: The Emergence of Liberty in the West

Format: CD (24)

Resource for: Age 14 to adult

Subjects: History, American Government, Theology, Law

The Best of the Witherspoon School of Law and Public Policy

This audio curriculum recorded at the Witherspoon School of Law features some of the "best" messages by Doug Phillips, Howard Phillips, Chief Justice Roy Moore, Dr. Paul Jehle, Dr. Joseph Morecraft III, Larry Pratt, and more. Some of the topics included are:

The Ten Commandments on Trial

Biblical Ethics for Public Policy

Biblical Law, Natural Law, or Positive Law

How to Combat the Lawless Social Worker Establishment

The Role of Church Courts

Format: CD (16)

Resource for: Age 14 to adult

Subjects: History, American Government, Theology, Law

An Encouragement: The materials reviewed from the Witherspoon School of Law and Public Policy can be used as a high school or college curriculum supplement. Fascinating to watch and listen to, these talks are designed for students with an interest in law from a biblical perspective. The topics are timely and relevant, and an excellent resource for your homeschool curriculum if approached with the necessary maturity to appreciate the expertise of the speakers. The additional resources reviewed below make an excellent complement to the Witherspoon materials, and are also appropriate for stand-alone studies.

The Importance of the Electoral College

Most children do not realize that the candidate for U.S. President who receives the most votes does not necessarily win the election. Because of the Electoral College, our country has a unique system that provides extra safeguards against majority tyranny. This book by Dr. George Grant explains the four reasons behind the Framers' decision to create an Electoral College, as well as detailing the makeup of that body and the way in which electors are appointed by states. This is a very helpful handbook for those who either don't know what the Electoral College is, or who do know and are wondering whether it should still exist.

Format: Book

Resource for: Age 12 to adult

Subjects: American Government, Law, History

How to Dethrone the Imperial Judiciary

The United States government consists of three branches; the legislative, the judicial, and the executive. As a part of the checks and balances implemented by our Founding Fathers, the judicial branch does not have the right to make law, only to interpret it and to apply it to specific cases. Sadly, the courts have become loaded with activist judges bent only on their own agendas, and not the laws of their country, for which purposes they blatantly misinterpret the Constitution, and rely heavily on foreign law for their decisions. Dr. Edwin Vieira outlines this problem in Part One of *How to Dethrone the Imperial Judiciary* by dealing specifically with the case of *Lawrence vs. Texas*. Part Two studies the ways in which the states, Congress, and the President can restrict and punish the imperial judiciary's wrongful application of United States law.

Format: Book

Resource for: Age 14 to adult

Subjects: American Government, Law, History

An Encouragement: The Importance of the Electoral College and How to Dethrone the Imperial Judiciary *provide the insight and knowledge needed to properly understand our governmental systems. Both should be read by any young man before leaving home.*

Biblical Principles of the Ballot Box

This thought-provoking message by Doug Phillips outlines the common perspective of Christians today toward voting the "lesser of two evils," and only looking for "conservative values" instead of true biblical principles in the platform of a candidate. Because God's Word applies to every area of life, we must use a scriptural grid when analyzing political candidates. Mr. Phillips does not seek to promote one particular candidate or party, but instead speaks to the conscience of the church, raising and answering the question of "by what standard," and discussing the harmful consequences of not voting according to God's Law.

Format: CD

Resource for: Family

Subjects: American Government, Law, History

An Encouragement: What better way to discuss the voting process than by addressing the biblical issues associated with this privilege and responsibility? Not only a resource that can be used to study government and history, but also should be listened to before any county, state, or presidential election.

Additional Vision Forum Resources

Independence Day: Lessons from King Hezekiah on Freedom and Independence (CD), by Doug Phillips

The State of Parental Rights in America

In case after case, Child Protective Services has exercised scare tactics, aggressive interviewing, and gross disregard of the rights of parents. Don Hart, a Texas lawyer who has founded an organization to defend families, delivers an eye-opening lecture about the social services mindset and mode of procedure, focusing primarily on the 1983 McMartin Preschool Trial, and the more recent large-scale removal of children from a cult's ranch in El Dorado, Texas. The information presented is very concerning, but immensely helpful for homeschooling parents who do not want their children ripped from their home by potentially abusive social workers.

Format: DVD

Resource for: Parents and young adults

Subjects: American Government, Law, Theology

An Encouragement: We must never take for granted the right we have to home educate our children. Watch this DVD to be sure you are guarding your home properly. Be mindful of the need to retain the rights so valiantly fought for by those who have gone before us.

Glory, Duty and the Gold Dome

Fourteen-year-old Thomas and his father, Georgia State Representative, John Richards, are working together on John's congressional campaign. Mr. Richards knows that the firm biblical principles he holds are necessary for a solid nation, and he's ready to help bring about a much-needed change in the political world. When a horrible car crash leaves a pregnant young woman in a coma, the father-son team unite to fight a legal battle against unprincipled men, including the young woman's husband, who want to remove her from life support. *Glory, Duty and the Gold Dome,* written by T. Nathaniel Darnell, is full of action and suspense as Thomas and his father work together in the face of mounting odds to do what is right, regardless of the political cost.

Format: Book

Resource for: Age 14 to adult

Subjects: American Government, Literature, Theology

Glory, Duty and the Gold Dome provides an extremely helpful overview of the legislative system, and the various steps followed by lawmakers. The author, T. Nathaniel Darnell, served as a legislative aide for many years, gaining a unique perspective on the inner workings of our modern political system. An excellent way to reinforce the concepts communicated in this book is to take a field trip to your local state capitol, touring the facilities and learning more about your state history.

The Art of Film

One of the most challenging aspects of parenthood for my husband and me has been discerning how to protect our children from the societal evils that would so quickly seek to devour them, and yet, at the same time, prepare them to not only function well in society, but to be sharp as arrows ready to pierce the fallacies of their generation. As a mother, I have found films and filmmaking an area to be entered with caution. Attending the San Antonio Christian Independent Film Festival, and then partaking of the resources stemming from that event, has done much to enlighten my understanding of the value of this communication medium. The book *Outside Hollywood* has had perhaps the greatest impact on my willingness to address filmmaking and movies as a part of my curriculum. Realizing the powerful impact films have on our culture, I wanted my family to understand this influence from both a positive and negative perspective so as to be prepared to participate in the battle of the worldviews. I urge you to consider using some of the materials included in this section in your curriculum. These resources can be applied in the form of language arts, history and career education studies, as well as photography and the actual technical process of filmmaking. A personal caution: as a part of the pursuit of any process of Christian filmmaking, I would first ensure that sound theology and a proper biblical worldview is included in my curriculum.

Outside Hollywood

Isaac Botkin has many years of filmmaking experience under his belt, from which he shares enthusiastically in this fascinating guide for Christians who want to operate outside of Hollywood. Starting by showing why filmmaking is a legitimate career for Christians, and the necessity of having a biblical worldview, Mr. Botkin discusses the history of Hollywood and how and why it arrived at its present level of moral degeneracy. Whether your child is interested in writing, directing, producing, or other aspects of film, this book will provide practical information and tips. An added plus is that the advice included in this book comes without having to sift through pages of pagan and defiling content. Even if your children are not interested in filmmaking, *Outside Hollywood* can help you to evaluate the kind of movies that should be watched, and why.

Format: Book

Resource for: Age 14 to adult

Subjects: History, Career Education, Photography, Art, Theology

Topics for Composition and Discussion

> Technical Aspects of Filmmaking
>
> Independent Filmmaking
>
> The Impact of Marxism on the Making of Films
>
> How Hollywood Has Impacted Our Culture

Further Study

> Animation
>
> Christian Pragmatism
>
> Digital Cameras
>
> Frankfort School
>
> Humanism
>
> Storyboards
>
> Marxism

The following Vision Forum resources can be used as complementary to, or as a more in-depth study on, the topic of Christian filmmaking.

From Script to Cinema

The visual arts have long been subjected to Hollywood's evil, anti-God culture. Modern films are full of profanity, immorality, and extremely unbiblical principles. But hope is on the horizon. A new generation of filmmakers is rising up, prepared to battle Hollywood's worldview and present their own theology instead. *From Script to Cinema* is a 10-DVD series designed to lay a foundational understanding of the biblical theology of filmmaking, as well as provide useful advice concerning its technical aspects. The following topics are included:

Biblical Worldview and Theology for Christian Filmmakers

The Deformation and Reformation of the Arts

Making a Short Film

Hands-on Lighting and 16mm Film Techniques

Copyright and Trademark Issues for Filmmakers

Format: DVD (10)

Resource for: Age 12 to adult

Subjects: History, Career Education, Art, Theology

Lights, Camera, Action! 2009 Christian Film Academy

Doug Phillips, Geoff and Isaac Botkin, James Finn, Dean Jones, and Stephen Kendrick all joined together in January 2009 to teach film students about the movie-making process. In this audio collection from the event, each man brings a unique background and skill level to the podium, ensuring maximum benefit to the listener. Topics range from principles of photography and biblical representations of violence to lighting and common mistakes.

Format: CD (20)

Resource for: Age 12 to adult

Subjects: Career Education, Art, Theology

History Has Been Made: Moments and Messages from the 2009 SAICFF

The 2009 San Antonio Independent Christian Film Festival included a variety of talks by men such as Doug Phillips, Geoff Botkin, Kevin

Swanson, Kirk Cameron, Stephen Kendrick, and Dean Jones. The topics included in this audio series from that event feature a discussion on narration and the arts for the glory of God, a behind-the-scenes look at *Fireproof*, entrepreneurial principles in filmmaking, and even a musical tribute to the Reformation!

Format: CD (14)

Resource for: Age 10 to adult

Subjects: Career Education, Art, Theology

Walt Disney: A Christian Critique

Perhaps no man in the twentieth century has had such an impact on the culture of family, both for good and for evil, as Walt Disney. Millions of boys and girls grew up watching *Mickey Mouse, Snow White, Pinocchio*, and dozens of other Disney films. Because Walt Disney was always so far ahead of the competition in technical quality and story structure, his movies became the much-loved classics that parents still want to share with their children today. Regrettably, he based the content of his stories on an often flawed and indefinable moral code. As Christian filmmakers, there is much that can be learned both from his successes and failures. The following topics are included:

Symposium on Disney, Film, and American Culture: A Theological Critique

Doug Phillips begins this three-part series with an interesting and concise overview of Disney's life and works, as well as an intense discussion on his strengths, weaknesses, and impact on the culture.

The Life and Times of Walt Disney: Understanding Walt's 1899 Ethical Default Position

Geoff Botkin demonstrates that, because Walt Disney had no real basis for his code of morality, he would default to a certain ethical standard. The moral decline in his films can be traced to the growth of his company and a changing worldview.

The Rise and Fall of the Disney Studio: The Objective Pursuit of Quality in the Development of Art and Story

Isaac Botkin explores the gradual increase of quality in Disney's films, as well as its inevitable moral decline, as his company increased in size and Walt had less personal contact with the individual movies.

Format: CD (3)

Resource for: Age 12 to adult

Subjects: History, Career Education, Art

Christianity and Science Fiction: Reclaiming the Genre for Christ

Humanists and evolutionists have taken captive the science fiction genre, and it's up to Christians to stop them! In this DVD, Doug Phillips looks at the types of science fiction films made in the last 100 years and the varying levels of evolution, mysticism, and socialism they have expressed. Learn the difference between "hard sci-fi" and "fantasy sci-fi," the reason for fims' extra-terrestrial tendencies, the movement of modern scientism towards mysticism, and much more. Some of the movies discussed are *Metropolis, Star Trek, Star Wars, Contact, Gattaca,* and *Indiana Jones and the Kingdom of the Crystal Skull.*

Format: DVD (1) and, CD (2)

Resource for: Age 12 to adult

Subjects: History, Career Education, Art

An Encouragement: *After viewing this film, have your family write your own theology of science fiction. Why not encourage your children to write a script for a science fiction movie that is faithful to biblical standards?*

Additional Vision Forum Resources

Jonathan Park Vol. I: The Adventure Begins (4 CDs):

#3: *"The Escape from Utopia"*

Outside Hollywood (book), by Isaac Botkin

Hollywood vs. Christian Culture Collection

Our culture has been subjugated by Hollywood. In order to release it from the bonds of ungodly, immoral, and sensual captivity, we must establish a firm foundation and overarching vision for movies that glorify God and exalt his principles. To fill this void, Doug Phillips, Geoff Botkin, and R.C. Sproul Jr. teamed up to provide a biblical vision for filmmaking. Included in this collection are:

Hollywood's Most Despised Villain

Geoff. Botkin gives a comprehensive history of the takeover of

Hollywood by Marxists and their battle to destroy biblical patriarchy. He also defines holiness, aesthetics, and antithesis, and discusses the Frankfort School's use of the sensuality cartel in modern America.

What Must Happen: A Christian Vision of Film and Culture

Doug Phillips provides a tremendous visionary outlook on the state of film today, and the necessary steps Christians must take in order to reclaim this powerful medium. We have an amazing opportunity to make movies for the glory of God!

The Priority Elements for the New Independent Christian Film Industry

It is not enough to know the problems with Hollywood; we must be able to do something about them. In other words, we must create our own independent Christian film industry. In this lecture, Geoff Botkin shares ten necessary elements for this new movement.

What Hollywood Knows that You Don't, and What You Know that Hollywood Doesn't

Because Hollywood has been making movies for so long, they have many of the technical skills that rising Christian filmmakers do not. However, they do not have the proper vision to use those skills. Mr. Botkin presents and expounds upon ten important disciplines that Hollywood has mastered, and which Christians must also achieve, in order to make technically excellent films.

The Weapons of Our Warfare: Truth

Our culture of postmodernism will not accept an objective standard of truth, but we as Christians know that Jesus Christ is our Truth. Dr. R.C. Sproul Jr. argues that it is our duty to make films that reflect this principle, but in a way that supports the story instead of turning every movie into a sermon.

The Weapons of Our Warfare: Beauty

Hollywood filmmakers have technical skills, but they lack a true understanding of beauty, something that Christians have been given through God's holy inspired Word. Dr. R.C. Sproul Jr. explains that we don't need to copy the culture; we need to create a new one.

Format: CD (6)

Resource for: Age 14 to adult

Subjects: History, Theology, Career Education, Art, Worldview

Power Tools for Future Filmmakers and Culture Changers

Is filmmaking a legitimate vocation for Christians? If so, how involved should we be? What are the dangers against which we must guard ourselves? This audio set answers these questions and many more. Speakers Geoff Botkin and Rich Christiano are both skilled filmmakers who have made many movies over their long careers, and are willing to share their insights with a new, "epistemologically self-confident" generation. Included in this collection are:

Vocational Realities for Aspiring Filmmakers

Geoffrey Botkin provides scriptural warrant for filmmaking as a career for Christians, while warning of the inherent dangers of this vocation. He offers perspective on how to develop vision and how to get started with small family productions.

Symposium on Creating Scripts that Glorify God

The script is the skeleton of your film. Without a skeleton, the human body will fall apart, and we've seen this happen with many modern films that have relied on special effects and stylistic camera techniques, instead of using a quality script. Geoff Botkin cautions that without a well-planned, God-glorifying script, your movie may as well end up in the dumpster as the movie theatre.

How to Finance and Distribute a Christian Film

Ideas are easy to get; it's the cold hard cash that doesn't come so quickly. You may have the necessary theological grounding, and even a worthwhile script, but without financing it's nearly impossible to get the cameras rolling, and without distributing power your work has been a waste of time. Rich Christiano has written, and directed multiple feature films, and he shares a successful model for finance and distribution.

A Step-by-Step Look at Producing an Independent Christian Film

One of Rich Christiano's films is entitled *Time Changer*, which explores the dangers of teaching moralistic values without mentioning Christ. Mr. Christiano leads listeners step-by-step through the process of directing and producing *Time Changer*, giving advice and direction to those who wish to follow in his path.

The Twelve Most Common Mistakes of Beginning Directors

It has been said that the best way to learn is through mistakes. Wouldn't it be nice to learn from those of others? Geoff Botkin not only outlines frequently-made mistakes, but gives practical advice to change them into successes. Learn from those who have gone before you.

Format: CD (5)

Resource for: Age 14 to adult

Subjects: Career Education, Art

Can the Western be Saved from the Hollywood Marxists?

The Western is a quintessential film genre. Gunslingers, sheriffs, stampedes, and broncos are all part of this rough-and-tumble tradition. Today's westerns are full of nihilistic principles and twisted morals, presenting weak fathers, broken families, and successful outlaws. Join Geoff Botkin and Doug Phillips as they travel through the history of westerns, detailing the gradual decline of moral values and the originally subtle Marxist influences to which audiences have been subjected.

Format: CD

Resource for: Age 14 to adult

Subjects: History, Theology, Worldview

San Antonio Independent Christian Film Festival Triple Album set 2004-2006

The San Antonio Independent Christian Film Festival exists to provide a forum of instruction and distribution for Christ-honoring filmmakers who will not compromise in their message by allowing Hollywood to dictate their morality. This set contains some of the best submissions to the 2004, 2005, and 2006 festivals, including dramas, documentaries, stop-motion animation, and more.

Format: DVD (15)

Resource for: Family

Subjects: History, Theology, Art

Business & Commerce

The materials presented in this section will help your family focus on how to develop a vision of spiritual and economic fruitfulness. You will be encouraged in the managing, investing, and creative use of your assets and resources.

Discovering Life Purpose

This message is a helpful resource for everyone seeking God's purpose for their life. Doug Phillips warns against reliance on humanistic tools such as personality profiles, instead encouraging us to look to the principles and precepts of Scripture as guided by God's Holy Spirit. Mr. Phillips breaks down the process of discovering life purpose by explaining that there are three distinct levels: general, gender-directed, and personal.

Format: CD

Resource for: Age 12 to adult

Subjects: Career Education, Theology

Topics for Composition and Discussion

How does Psalm One apply to making life decisions?

Why it is necessary to have a multigenerational vision for family to know life purpose?

How does honoring parents help to determine life purpose?

Further Study

Precepts

Principles

Multigenerational Vision

Egalitarianism

The Best of the Entrepreneurial Bootcamp for Christian Families

This compilation of messages from the 2006 Entrepreneurial Bootcamp provides more than twenty hours of practical and philosophical encouragement for everyone interested in Christian entrepreneurship. A number of Christian men with a wide range of entrepreneurial experience address a variety of helpful topics such as, "Building a Business from Start to Finish," "Fathers and Sons Working Together," and "Creative Models for Raising Capital without Debt Bondage." Learn how Christian entrepreneurship can, and must, emphasize multigenerational faithfulness, inheritance, jurisdiction, and the household as a vibrant, productive unit for cultural transformation.

Format: CD (20)

Resource for: Age 12 to adult

Subjects: Career Education, Business, Home Economics

An Encouragement: A streamlined version of this audio collection is also available on DVD. Both the audio and video versions provide hours of instruction on how to build a business, from the spiritual aspects to the legal issues. The applications are endless, both for practical life skills and projects pertaining to the requirements of any business course. And on top of all of this, the messages are just fun to listen to!

Biblical Economics: A Complete Study Course

This set consists of the book *Biblical Economics*, written by R.C. Sproul Jr., together with a course syllabus; a free electronic copy of Frederic Bastiat's classic work, *The Law*, and David Chilton's, *Productive Christians in an*

Age of Guilt Manipulators; a comprehensive study guide, and 12 audio lectures. The book is a treasure trove of basic economic concepts viewed through the lens of Scripture. The warnings against, and treatment, of debt and government spending are incredibly relevant in our society today, and the time you spend learning about economic principles such as wealth creation and inflation will be truly profitable.

Format: Book, E-books (2), CD Audio Lectures (12), Study Guide, Syllabus

Resource for: Age 14 to adult

Subjects: Economics, Theology

An Encouragement: This course is great to do as a family! Not only does it provide economic insight and expertise for your personal economy, it can also be used as a tool to prepare your children for their economic future.

APPENDIX A:
CHRONOLOGICAL & TOPICAL UNIT STUDIES WITH RESOURCES

CREATION AND EARLY WORLD HISTORY

History of the World (10 DVDs):

> #2: "The World That Perished," by Dr. John Whitcomb

History of the World: B.C. (20 CDs):

> #3: "A Defense of the Universality of the Genesis Flood," by Dr. John Whitcomb

> #4: "The Implications of the Genesis Flood on Earth History," by Dr. John Whitcomb

Mysteries of the Ancient World (12 CDs):

> #4, 5, 6: "The Mystery of the Nephilim Presented and Solved," by Doug Phillips

History of the World: B.C. (20 CDs):

> #8: "The Tower of Babel and the Dispersion of the Nations," by Dr. John Whitcomb
>
> #20: "The Long War Against God," by Dr. John Whitcomb
>
> #6: "The History of the Ice Age," by Dr. John Morris
>
> #9: "One Blood: The Origin of the Races," by Dr. John Morris
>
> #10: "The Puzzle of Ancient Man," by Doug Phillips
>
> #11: "Controversies in Biblical Chronology," by Dr. Floyd Jones

Mysteries of the Ancient World (12 CDs):

> #1: "The Cosmic Implications of Creation Ex Nihilo," by Doug Phillips

ROME

History of the World: B.C. (20 CDs):

> #17: "The Meaning of Rome," by Dr. George Grant

Providential Battles Vol. 1 (4 CDs):

> #1: "Cannae," by William Potter (216 B.C.)

The Young Carthaginian (book), by G.A. Henty (220 B.C.)

History of the World: A.D. (20 CDs):

> #7: "The Battle of Teutoburg Forest," by Col. John Eidsmoe (9 A.D.)

Beric the Briton (book), by G.A. Henty (A.D. 61)

For the Temple (book), by G.A. Henty (A.D. 70)

History of the World: A.D. (20 CDs):

> #4: "The Rise of Byzantium and the Fall of Rome", by Dr. George Grant
>
> #5, 6: "How Augustine Changed the World," Pts. 1 & 2, by Dr. Joseph Morecraft III

MIDDLE AGES

History of the World: A.D. (20 CDs):

> #8: "The Problem With Medieval Scholasticism," by Dr. Joseph

Morecraft III

Providential Battles: Vol. 1 (4 CDs):

#1: "Tours," by William Potter (732)

History of the World (10 DVDs):

#5: "Vikings: Their Law, Culture, and Conquests," by Col. John Eidsmoe

The Dragon and the Raven (book), by G.A. Henty (870)

The Norseman in the West (book), by R.M. Ballantyne (c. 1000)

Wulf the Saxon (book), by G.A. Henty (1066)

History of the World (10 DVDs):

#6: "The Crusades," by Dr. George Grant

Winning His Spurs (book), by G.A. Henty (1190)

St. George for England (book), by G.A. Henty (1340)

Providential Battles: Vol. 1 (4 CDs):

#2: "Crecy," (1346), "Constantinople," (1453), by William Potter

The Lion of St. Mark (book), by G.A. Henty (1380)

Both Sides of the Border (book), by G.A. Henty (1400)

At Agincourt (book), by G.A. Henty (1415)

Sabers, Spears, & Catapults (4 CDs):

#2: "Agincourt: Longbows, Swords, and the End of an Era," by William Potter

A Knight of the White Cross (book), by G.A. Henty (1480)

ANCIENT SCOTLAND AND HER BATTLE FOR FREEDOM

How the Scots Saved Christendom (12 CDs):

#1: "Overview of Scottish History," by Phillips, Potter, & Morecraft

#9: "The Isle of Iona," by Phillips, Potter, & Morecraft

#5: "Tales from Bannockburn," by Philips, Potter, & Strackbein

#6: "Tribute: The William Wallace Monument," by Phillips & Potter

In Freedom's Cause (book), by G.A. Henty (1314)

Both Sides of the Border (book), by G.A. Henty (1400)

MAYAS, INCAS, AND AZTECS

History of the World (10 DVDs):

> #7: "The Message of the Mayas," by Doug Phillips

Mysteries of the Ancient World (12 CDs):

> #9, 10, 11: "The Mystery of the Incas: Machu Picchu and the Lost Legacy of the Stone Masons," by Doug Phillips

By Right of Conquest (book), by G.A. Henty (1595)

Providential Battles: Vol. 1 (4 CDs):

> #2: "Tenochtitlan," by William Potter (1521)

Mysteries of the Ancient World (12 CDs):

> #7, 8: "The Mystery of the Ica Stones and the Nazca Lines: Dragon Riders and Owl Men," by Doug Phillips

THE REFORMATION

History of the World: A.D. (20 CDs):

> #9: "What Every Christian Needs to Know about the Reformation," by Dr. Joseph Morecraft III

> #2: "A Brief History of Martyrdom, Persecution, and Inquisition," by Dr. Joseph Morecraft III

Christianity and Western Civilization (10 DVDs):

> #1: "Five Hundred Years of Liberty Birthed by the Reformation," by Doug Phillips

> #5: "The Influence of the Reformation on Global Exploration and Warfare," by William Potter

> #6: "The Reformation Influence on Art and Culture," by Doug Phillips

> #9: "Competing Views of Dominion: Roman Catholic vs. Reformed," by Dan Ford

Reformers & Revolutionaries (10 DVDs):

> #5: "Calvin's Spiritual Forefathers: The Men Who Paved the Way

for the Reformation," by Marcus Serven

#1: "In Defense of the 'Solas' of the Reformation," by Dr. Joseph Morecraft III

#9: "The Reformers and the Paper Trail of Freedom," by Marshall Foster

#6: "Martin Luther," by R.C. Sproul Jr.

St. Bartholomew's Eve (book), by G.A. Henty (1570)

Reformers & Revolutionaries (10 DVDs):

#10: "Lessons from the Waldenses," by Geoff Botkin

Reformation and Revival (book), by John Brown

By Pike and Dyke (book), by G.A. Henty (1579)

Under Drake's Flag (book), by G.A. Henty (1580)

By England's Aid (book), by G.A. Henty (1588)

Providential Battles: Vol. 1 (4 CDs):

#2: "Armada," (1588) by William Potter

JOHN CALVIN

John Calvin: Man of the Millennium (book), by Philip Volmer

Christianity & Western Civilization (10 DVDs):

#2: "The Man of the Millennium," by Dr. Joseph Morecraft III

History of the World: A.D. (20 CDs):

#10: "The Global Influence of John Calvin," by Dr. Joseph Morecraft III

Christianity & Western Civilization (10 DVDs):

#4: "The Bible Unleashed: Calvin's Role in Producing the Geneva Bible," by Marshall Foster

Reformers & Revolutionaries (10 DVDs):

#8: "Calvin's Doctrine of Worship," by Dr. Joseph Morecraft III

#7: "John Calvin on the Biblical Doctrine of the Family," by Scott Brown

#3: "John Calvin's View of Law," by Dr. Joseph Morecraft III

Christianity & Western Civilization (10 DVDs):

#7: "Calvin and Darwin: The Impact of Friendships on Civilization," by Doug Phillips

JOHN KNOX

Reformers & Revolutionaries (10 DVDs):

#2: "Spare No Arrows: The Life and Legacy of John Knox," by Wesley Strackbein

How the Scots Saved Christendom (12 CDs):

#3: "The Impact of John Knox," by Phillips, Morecraft, & Strackbein

#8: "Wishart's Martyrdom and Knox's Rise," by Phillips, Morecraft, & Strackbein

EARLY AMERICAN SETTLEMENT

History of the World (10 DVDs):

#9: "The Miracle of America," by Dr. Marshall Foster

#8: "America's Four Hundredth Birthday: Jamestown's Legacy of Law and Gospel," by Doug Phillips

A Comprehensive Defense of the Providence of God (21 DVDs):

#2: "The Providential Beginnings of America," by Dr. Paul Jehle

#3: "The Panorama of Providence at Jamestown," by Stephen McDowell

#8: "Warfare: The Powhatans vs. the Englishmen," by William Potter

From Jamestown to Jubilee: The Virginia Faith & Freedom Tour (1 MP3 or 9 CDs):

#1, 2: "Jamestown Island, Captain John Smith," by Doug Phillips

Jamestown: Ancient Landmark, Modern Battleground (DVD)

A Comprehensive Defense of the Providence of God (21 DVDs):

#4: "The Life of Captain John Smith," by Doug Phillips

#7: "Jamestown and the Puritans," by Dr. Joseph Morecraft III

The Providential Nexus of Jamestown and Plymouth (DVD), by Dr. Paul Jehle

To Have and To Hold (book), by Mary Johnston

Reformers & Revolutionaries (10 DVDs):

> #4: "John Robinson: Shepherd of America," by Paul Jehle

Landmarks and Liberty: The New England Faith & Freedom Tour (1 MP3 or 9 CDs)

Of Plymouth Plantation (book), by William Bradford

Christianity & Western Civilization (10 DVDs):

> #8: "How Calvinism Built New England, How New England Built America," by Paul Jehle

> #10: "The Use of Biblical Law in the American Colonies," by Col. John Eidsmoe

A Comprehensive Defense of the Providence of God (21 DVDs):

> #5: "The Coming of the Bible to America," by Dr. Marshall Foster

Pilgrims vs. Indians (CD), by Doug Phillips

Puritans vs. Witches (CD), by Dr. Paul Jehle

SCOTLAND'S MARTYRS

How the Scots Saved Christendom (12 CDs):

> #8: "The Life and Impact of Samuel Rutherford," by Phillips, Potter, & Morecraft

> #8: "Patrick Hamilton: The Scottish Reformation's First Martyr," by Phillips & Potter

> #2: "The Covenanters' Memorial: The Market Cross," by Phillips, Potter, & Morecraft

> #2: "The Martyrs' Monument," by Phillips, Potter, & Morecraft

Hunted and Harried (book), by R.M. Ballantyne (1680's)

AMERICAN WAR FOR INDEPENDENCE, AND FOUNDING FATHERS

A Comprehensive Defense of the Providence of God (21 DVDs):

> #11: "Bacon's Rebellion: Our First War of Independence," by Col. John Eidsmoe

> #6: "The Literature of Freedom of Our Founding Fathers," by Dan Ford

Let Freedom Ring: The Philadelphia Faith & Freedom Tour (1 MP3 or 13 CDs)

Landmarks and Liberty: The New England Faith & Freedom Tour (1 MP3 or 9 CDs):

> #6, 7: "Lexington Green," Pts. I & II, and "Copp's Hill Burying Ground," Part I

A Comprehensive Defense of the Providence of God (21 DVDs):

> #17, 18: "The Providence and Perseverance of George Washington," Pts. I & II, by Dr. Peter Lillback

George Washington: America's Joshua (CD), by Doug Phillips

True to the Old Flag (book), by G.A. Henty (1776)

From Jamestown to Jubilee: The Virginia Faith & Freedom Tour (1 MP3 or 9 CDs):

> #5: "Patrick Henry," "Yorktown Battlefield," and "Mt. Vernon, Part I"

> #6: "Mt. Vernon, Part II," "Behind Mt. Vernon," and "Monticello"

Providential Battles: Vol. 2 (4 CDs):

> #2: "New York City," by William Potter (1776)

Providential Battles: Vol. 1 (4 CDs):

> #3: "Saratoga," (1777), and "Yorktown," (1781), by William Potter

Christians vs. Deists (CD), by Dr. Joseph Morecraft III

Patriots vs. Tories (CD), by Dr. Joseph Morecraft III

THE WAR BETWEEN THE STATES

Yankees vs. Rebels (CD), by William Potter

With Lee in Virginia (book), by G.A. Henty (1861)

Providential Battles: Vol. 1 (4 CDs):

> #4: "Antietam," by William Potter (1862)

Providential Battles: Vol. 2 (4 CDs):

> #2: "Gaines Mill," by William Potter (1862)

The Life and Campaigns of Stonewall Jackson (book), by Robert Louis Dabney

Christ in the Camp (book), by J. William Jones

EVANGELISM AND MISSIONARY ENDEAVORS

History of the World: A.D. (20 CDs):

#15: "Nineteenth-Century Missions," by William Potter

How the Scots Saved Christendom (12 CDs):

#7: "David Livingstone's Impact on Christendom," by Phillips & Barret

The Adventure of Missionary Heroism (book), by John C. Lambert

Missionary Patriarch (book), by John G. Paton

WORLD WARS I AND II

Sergeant York and the Great War (book), edited by Tom Skeyhill and "Little Bear" Wheeler

The League of Grateful Sons (DVD)

Coming In on a Wing and a Prayer (book), by Kelly Bradrick (née Brown)

Providential Battles: Vol. 1 (4 CDs):

#4: "1st Marne," (1914), "Britain," (1940), "Midway," (1942), and "Stalingrad," (1942-3) by William Potter

Providential Battles: Vol. 2 (4 CDs):

#4: "Normandy," by William Potter (1944)

DARWIN AND THE GALÁPAGOS

The Mysterious Islands (DVD)

Christianity & Western Civilization (10 DVDs):

#7: "Calvin and Darwin: The Impact of Friendships on Civilization," by Doug Phillips

Mysteries of the Ancient World (12 CDs):

#12, 13: "The Mystery of the Galápagos: Laboratory of Evolution or Testimony to Creation?" by Doug Phillips

Jonathan Park Goes to the Galápagos (4 CDs)

Darwin vs. Calvin: The Battle of the Millennium (DVD)

LIST OF ALBUMS USED FOR THESE STUDIES

History of the World (10 DVDs)

History of the World: B.C. (20 CDs)

History of the World: A.D. (20 CDs)

Providential Battles: Vol. 1 (4 CDs)

Providential Battles: Vol. 2 (4 CDs)

Sabers, Spears, and Catapults (4 CDs)

Mysteries of the Ancient World (12 CDs)

A Comprehensive Defense of the Providence of God (21 DVDs)

Reformers & Revolutionaries (10 DVDs)

Christianity & Western Civilization (10 DVDs)

How the Scots Saved Christendom (12 CDs)

From Jamestown to Jubilee: The Virginia Faith & Freedom Tour (1 MP3 or 9 CDs)

Landmarks and Liberty: The New England Faith & Freedom Tour (1 MP3 or 8 CDs)

Let Freedom Ring: The Philadelphia Faith & Freedom Tour (1 MP3 or 13 CDs)

Jonathan Park Goes to the Galápagos (4 CDs)

APPENDIX B:
ACADEMIC PLANS FOR THE USE OF VISION FORUM RESOURCES

UNIT STUDIES

Almost any item sold by Vision Forum can provide a framework for a unit study, whether you are studying the past or the present:

1. Preview a resource or watch/listen together as a family.

2. Select topics that would complement present or future areas of study.

3. Choose resources from Vision Forum and other sources such as your local library or the Internet.

4. Apply the knowledge learned through documentation:

    A. Discussion

    B. Writing projects

C. Arts and crafts

A textbook can be a resource, if needed, to provide factual information or a timeline, but always be careful to understand and discuss the worldview of the author and/or publisher.

When studying a particular era or topic in history, your study can be enhanced by the inclusion of other subjects. For example:

Geography

Maps of the area you are studying can be drawn and examined, and the geographical locations and topography can be considered to discern how the characteristics of an area impacted its history. The climate can also be considered to determine the influence of weather.

Science

Many people opt to focus on science apart form whatever other subject they are studying, but a unit study can include scientific discoveries and/or men of science who lived during the time being studied. It is fascinating to see how many of our scientific discoveries were made by men who used the Bible as their source book.

Language Arts

Note-taking, outlining, and defining words, can be applied to any CD listened to, DVD watched, or book read. Writing essays, position papers, journals, even a letter to grandma defining the lessons leaned through the resource can be a form of documentation. Finding Scripture verses to support positions or illustrate concepts makes Bible study meaningful. Poetry from the time period or about the topic being studied can be copied, or new, related poetry composed. The books, *Poetry for Patriarchs* and *Verses of Virtue,* are excellent resources for this. Speeches can be developed and delivered in costume or the personality of the character. Literature from the time period being studied can be read and reported upon, or just enjoyed and discussed through a read-aloud.

Government & Economics

How did the leaders and governments of this time period impact the people and circumstances? How was God accomplishing His providential purposes? The same points can be applied to economics.

Math

Are there any mathematicians of renown from this time period or country? Try studying some of the engineering feats that took place. The bridges, aqueducts, and methods of protection can all be addressed from a mathematical perspective.

Fine Arts

The composers, artists, and architectural styles can all be researched and their creations discussed as to how they reflect the culture of their time.

History

How has God used the events in this study to further His providential path in history? What insights can be gleaned about man and God from this study? How is God using your time of history in His plan?

Health and Physical Education

A study can be made of the nutrition, medicine, and health conditions of any time period. How does the health and physical activity of a nation impact its history? How do a people stay fit, and what, if any, is their mode of relaxation?

Textbook Courses

Many parents choose to use textbooks or pre-determined courses of study. Looking for resources that enhance this form of study, such as Vision Forum's *Christianity & Western Civilization* DVD serires, can provide insight and additional historical information about the workings of God's hand in history.

Online Courses

Some parents choose to use online courses as a means of providing instruction to their children. Vision Forum's resources can be used to complement these courses and to provide helpful perspective from a biblical worldview.

The Schooling of Every Day Life

We all have seasons of life where our best laid plans and goals seem to fall short. Sickness, pregnancy, the care of an elderly parent, a new business, or a family move can often change the style and mode of our education plan. Using CDs and DVDs to provide continued instruction when circumstances make life challenging can be a blessing.

On a Personal Note

Chores in our home have always been enhanced by listening to audio dramas, including *Jonathan Park*. Ironing and food preparation can become academic exercises when listening to history, church, and character resources. I still remember painting woodwork before the sale of a house and using that time to listen to the *Christian Controversies Collection*. And let us not forget vacations! *Landmarks and Liberty* and *How the Scots Saved Christendom* are a part of our travel memories.

INDEX OF
PRODUCT REVIEWS

C

D

E

F

G

H

I

J

L

M

N

O

P

R

S

Y